PALACES OF
Minoan Crete

Gerald Cadogan

with photographs by Lucy Cadogan
and drawings by Pat Clarke

METHUEN

London and New York

FOR LUCY

First published in 1976 by
Barrie & Jenkins Ltd

This corrected edition first published in 1980 by
Methuen & Co. Ltd
11 New Fetter Lane, London EC4P 4EE

Published in the USA by
Methuen & Co.
in association with Methuen, Inc.
733 Third Avenue, New York, NY 10017

© 1976 Gerald Cadogan

Printed in Great Britain by
J. W. Arrowsmith Ltd, Bristol

British Library Cataloguing in Publication Data
Cadogan, Gerald
    Palaces of Minoan Crete. – (University paperbacks).
    1. Minoans   2. Palaces – Crete
    I. Title   II. Series
    939.1′8   DF221.C8   79–41165

ISBN 0–416–73160–0

Contents

List of illustrations

Acknowledgements

I should like to thank the following institutions and persons who have kindly allowed me to use various illustrations:

The Visitors of the Ashmolean Museum, the Keeper of the Department of Antiquities and Dr H. W. Catling: Plates 4, 6, 7, 9, 11, 17; The Trustees of the British Museum, and Dr R. A. Higgins: Plate 5; The Managing Committee of the British School at Athens: Plates 3, 8, 46, 47; Dr P. M. Warren: Plate 2.

Other drawings of objects and plans have been re-drawn by Mrs Pat Clarke from original publications.

G.C.

Preface

We have known the Minoans now for almost three-quarters of a century, which happens to be about as long a time as that of the Mycenaean control of Knossos (c.1450–1375 B.C.). In these seventy-five years there has been much study and excavation, and we are always becoming better acquainted with them. This greater knowledge has not made them dull or stale. They are as fascinating now as they were to the pioneer archaeologists of Crete who came upon them at the beginning of the century.

The palaces and the country and town houses are the centres of Minoan civilisation. They are as important for our understanding of the Minoans as are their remarkable works of art on display in the Heraklion Museum. Too often however the buildings are dismissed with a quick glance as 'ruins'. This book is intended to reveal these buildings to the reader. It tries to give an account of how they have been built and, by pointing out the clues for reconstruction, how you can rebuild them yourself in your imagination. Only by such an effort can you develop a feeling for Minoan architecture, and for much of the Minoan way of living. This is what archaeologists have to do. The readers – and visitors – who try the same will comprehend better the processes of archaeology and, I hope, will find their enjoyment of Crete and the Minoans much enhanced.

The unity of Minoan architecture is not as immediately apparent as that of Classical Greek architecture; but it is there and, if you try to understand the buildings, you will find it. From such details as patterned floors or multiple doors you will learn the principles. You may be surprised by how similar Minoan architecture is to the twentieth-century reinforced concrete buildings of Greece, long and low, broken by columns for verandahs and terraces – a reminder perhaps that the problems of achieving an equable temperature and enough light without being baked by the sun are the same as they always were. Another problem that has not changed in Crete is that of coping with earthquakes: buildings must be given enough elasticity so that they do not fall down in the regular earthquakes. This is partly why the Minoans used timber-and-rubble construction, but even so Minoan buildings did often collapse. Today ferronconcrete is used, but you will see timber-and-rubble in fairly modern buildings of the time of the Turkish rule in Khania, Rethymno and Heraklion. In general you will find that the more you notice the traditional architecture of Crete, and particularly peasants' houses of the pre-concrete era, the more you will appreciate what the Minoans were doing. I have used the same sort of simple but efficient lavatory in a house near Palaikastro as was devised centuries ago for the Queen's apartments at Knossos.

The palaces are the expressions of the culture, religion and economy of the Minoans, and I should like to add 'and also of their personalities'; but personality is something we cannot learn from prehistory. Prehistory consists of history without literature, which accordingly restricts any judgements about the character of prehistoric people to obvious and simple generalisations. If we wonder what went on in the Minoan palaces and what the palaces contained and what that represents, we have nothing but our imaginations to guide us. Some of the facts about the Minoans are startling, and there are many contradictions: the palaces are not surrounded by defence walls; Minoan art can be both formal and naturalistic at the same time. When you recognise the contradictions, the Minoans begin to live.

In transliterating Greek names, I have several times chosen the most common names of sites, rather than been strictly consistent. In capitalising the names of rooms I have tried to be as consistent as possible in following what the excavators themselves have done.

This book has taken a long time to write for which I apologize to the publishers and commend their patience. I am very grateful to the many Cretans and lovers of Crete who have helped me by sharing their knowledge and ideas, or by showing me and letting me mention their finds. I should especially like to thank Mr Peter Megaw who suggested I write this book; Professor Nikolaos Platon for a magical tour of Zakro; Mrs Pat Clarke for her skill in making the drawings and her patience; and my wife Lucy for her photographs and for ensuring that the book was written.

Cincinnati   Gerald Cadogan

P.S.
Since the book was finished early in 1974, there are a few changes to be made which it is difficult to incorporate in the text: the date for the transition from Late Minoan IIIB to IIIC should be 1190, or even slightly later, rather than the round 1200; pottery of the Old Palaces has now been found as far up the Nile as Aswan; and I am much less certain that the rulers of Minoan Crete until 1450 were men, whether kings, priests or gods, or any or all combined, rather than women. (For Mycenaean Crete of 1450–1375 the Linear B tablets show that men ruled.) Finally, the visitor will find that a few rooms of the Minoan buildings have been shut off, to prevent their being damaged. One can however usually still see them from outside, and so I have left them in the text unaltered.

G.C.

1 The Origins of Minoan Civilisation

Crete

The island of Crete separates the Aegean Sea from the Libyan (Fig. 1), with its largest town, Heraklion, at 35° 20′ latitude and 25° 08′ longitude. Crete is placed between three continents. To the South, Africa is only some 250 km. away. To the East lie Rhodes and the mainland of Asia Minor, and Cyprus and Syria. West and North-West of Crete is mainland Greece, the last spur of continental Europe, and to the North the islands of the Aegean occupy the sea between Europe and Asia. Crete, on their southern limit, is by far the largest (Fig. 2).

From East to West, Crete is about 200 km. long (Fig. 4, p. 24). Its breadth from North to South varies from 12.5 km. at the isthmus of Ierapetra to 58 km. at its widest across Psiloriti in the centre. Nowhere does it take much more than a day to walk across. The island is composed of a series of mountain ranges, Psiloriti (or Mount Ida, 2456 m.) and the Lasithi mountains (often called Mount Dikte, 2148 m.) in the centre, Modhi in the East and the White Mountains (2452 m.) in the West. These mountains are mainly limestone. Their basic colour is grey. They are pervious to water and are eroded into the sharp outlines, ridges and precipices, gorges, caves and swallow-holes (Plate 1) and small upland plains and plateaux which characterise so much of Crete today. The upland plains are a special feature of Crete. They occur at 1000 m. high or more. The largest is the plain of Lasithi which is well worth visiting, but even it measures only 12 by 6 km.; others to see are Nidha on the North slopes of Psiloriti and Omalo in the White Mountains. The Lasithi plain often has snow in winter and is flooded until the water drains away into swallow-holes. It was first tilled by the Minoans who settled round the edge. They also used its caves as shrines, as some caves in Greece are still used today, and for burials.

The Cretan mountains are wild and beautiful and always surprise. They are both high and yet near the sea, which produces a remarkable variety of scenery in a small area. On the North coast you find rich and rolling slopes and foothills by the sea, but on the South the mountains are more sheer, though there are tiny plains at the foot of the seasonal watercourses. As for rivers, there are only five in Crete which are perennial. The beaches on the North coast are mostly sandy: on the South they have pebbles if they are below mountains. On both sides there are many small promontories which give enough protection for boats to be pulled up on the beach.

Crete's weather is warm to hot during most months of the year. The summer continues till December, tempered only by occasional rain after the autumn equinox, and from November the island begins to turn green. It is most green in

1   The gorge of Zakro, one of several gorges in the Cretan mountains.

Fig. 1.   Map of the East Mediterranean.

April when the wild flowers are at their best. In winter it is not cold – to a North European – but damp, which you notice more than at home, being less protected in Cretan houses. On the high ground snow falls in these months but nowhere does it lie throughout the year.

Winds in Crete blow off the sea: the North wind, the *meltemi* in summer, is a light breeze after sunrise which blows always harder till two or three o'clock in the afternoon, dying away at sunset. Often it becomes a gale and makes the sea very rough: and sometimes it even blows right over the tops of the mountains and, rushing down the South slopes, drives the sea away from the shore – the Venetians called this wind the *tramontana*. Occasionally a hot, parching dusty South wind blows from Libya for two or three days on end. This happens particularly in the spring, but it can come in the summer when it is hot to the point of being extremely unpleasant. One famous occasion when the South wind was blowing was when the palace of Knossos was destroyed about 1375 B.C. as one can see from the direction of the marks of burning on the West facade of the building.

Since antiquity the island has risen in places in the West and has sunk in the East. At its West end for instance the Roman harbourworks at Phalasarna are now up on dry land, and elsewhere the old shore line can be seen about 2 to 8 m. above the present one. At the other end Mokhlos, a Minoan settlement, is now an offshore island though it probably used to be a peninsular. Another change since antiquity, and a more important one, has been the loss of trees. This has led to a decline in rainfall and in agricultural potential; rivers have shrunk into streams, and many of the mountainous areas of the island have slowly been turned into wasteland. Destructive nibbling by goats has aggravated the losses caused by man.

The most prosperous periods in Crete's history appear to have been the Minoan and the Roman and, we can add, today. These are the times when settlements have been most dense, and only then – as now – have there been sufficiently long periods of peace to enable people to live on the low hills and flat land by the sea without needing fortifications. Today with a population of 422,198 (1971) the island is self-sufficient in basic foodstuffs, and exports a surplus of oranges, grapes, currants, wine and olive oil. There are still large flocks of sheep and goats: the most recent total of sheep in Crete is 529,910, and there were probably as many in Minoan times. The Knossos Linear B tablets record numbers of over 1,000 for single flocks of sheep, and likewise plenty of goats.

Apart from food, the island has few raw materials. Its limestones were used in building, and the walls and floors of the palaces and country houses were faced with gypsum, which is found in outcrops near most of the Minoan centres (the hill of Gypsades immediately south of the palace of Knossos is made of it). Serpentine, stalactite and breccia were stones often used for vases; and Crete also has a kind of marble, but the Minoans do not seem to have favoured it. One stone which they had to import was obsidian, a black, glassy stone of volcanic origin found in lumps on the beaches of Melos, 135 km. away to the North-West (Fig. 2). Already in the seventh millennium B.C. the earliest Neolithic people of Knossos had discovered how to use it for knapping into knives and blades, and the Minoans followed them. Later other varieties of obsidian came into fashion: a translucent type from Asia Minor, and one flecked with white spots and used by the Minoans for vases from the small island of Yiali (or 'Glass') off Kalimnos in the Dodecanese.

Copper surface deposits have been discovered recently in Crete, but they are small and were probably not enough for the Minoans' needs. In fact there is good reason to think they imported copper from Cyprus. Stores of copper ingots have been found at Ayia Triadha and at Zakro: at Zakro they were found in a room together with elephant tusks which would certainly have been imported since there is no evidence of elephants at any time in Crete. The tusks and the ingots could well have come to Zakro in the same boat together. Tin also had to be imported. It was as indispensable to the Bronze Age economy as oil is to ours: tin is an essential ingredient for making bronze. When it has been mixed with about nine times as much copper, the resulting bronze melts at a lower temperature, is easier to cast than pure copper and produces a harder product. Tin does not occur in Crete, nor anywhere nearer than Spain, the British Isles and Brittany, Central Europe, Etruria, Transcaucasia and Iran. Consequently (unless there were closer sources which have now been worked out) it had to come from one or other of these far-off places, doubtless through intermediaries. It is not surprising, then, that bronze does not appear regularly in Crete until relatively late in Minoan history in the second millennium. Before then arsenic and lead were sometimes used to alloy with copper, as they have a similar hardening effect to that of tin.

Luxuries like silver, gold, ivory, alabaster, carnelian, amethyst and lapis lazuli were among the other raw materials the Minoans imported. Most of these were introduced in the Early Minoan period, the third millennium, which is a small indication of how quickly the Minoans became civilised. Silver (and lead) probably came from the Cyclades, and ivory from Syria. In Middle Minoan times lapis lazuli arrived: it is a product of Afghanistan, probably introduced by or brought from the Syrians. Gold, alabaster and other semi-precious stones probably came from Egypt. Along with these raw materials were brought the products of the developed Eastern civilisations: scarab seals from Egypt, daggers from Byblos whose techniques had an influence on the local Cretan metalworking, and stone vases, beads and cylinder seals. Industrial and artistic techniques were introduced, such as the skills of faience, or of granulation (decorating with tiny grains) in goldsmithery. Curios and personal objects were imported. Several ostrich eggs have been found in the Aegean and, at Knossos, the statuette of an Egyptian called User who may have travelled there in the time of the Old Palaces. Many more things may have been imported which are now lost, rugs and cloth for example; and some artistic ideas doubtless came from abroad, perhaps the spiral which is so common a motif in Minoan art. It may have come from the Cyclades, while in the opposite direction many scenes on Minoan frescoes are clearly influenced by Egyptian wall paintings.

What did the Minoans send in return? Only a few of their products have been found abroad and certainly not enough to pay for all the imports. There are, for instance, some daggers in Cyprus, and stone vases in Syria and in the Aegean, and pottery, particularly the Kamares ware of the Old Palaces which travelled

Fig 2. Map of the South Aegean. The places marked by a star have many features of the Minoan way of life and may have been under Minoan control in the period of the New Palaces.

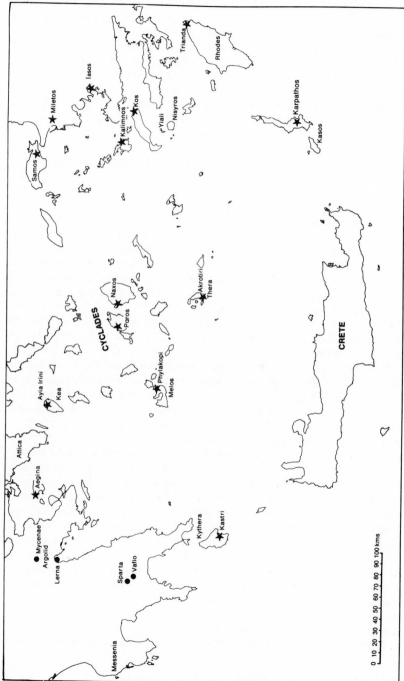

as far as Qatna in the upper Orontes valley and Abydos in Upper Egypt (Fig. 1). We are left to presume, however, that the staple Minoan exports would have been farm produce, since so few Minoan products have been identified outside Crete in the Near East or Egypt. Farm produce would have been especially valuable to Egypt which has always had a chronic lack of large-standing timber and of the products of vines and olives – they can only be grown there with difficulty. Minoan Crete may have exported cypress wood, as we know Crete did in Classical times, and wine, currants, olive oil, wool and cloth, and possibly herbs, which she sent to Europe in the eighteenth century A.D., and purple dye extracted from the *murex* shell. In time the Minoans may have also become agents for the export of metals from Central Europe to Egypt.

Now that we have seen something of the geographical and economic background of Minoan Crete, we can turn to the history of the Cretans. The first Cretans we know are the Early Neolithic people who settled on what was later the site of the palace of Knossos. Their first settlement (level X), perhaps a camp, was found 7 m. below the present surface of the Central Court. Nine other distinct building levels lay above it, each marking a stage of occupation when the earliest inhabitants of Knossos built or rebuilt their houses on the destroyed remains of the periods before. Archaeologists work out such a sequence of habitation by uncovering each level in turn and relating it to the others. The ten levels in the stratigraphy of Neolithic Knossos are the remains of about four thousand years of living before the Minoan culture began. A burnt oak stake from the 'camp' level X gives a Carbon-14 date of 6341 ± 180 B.C. (based on a half-life for Carbon-14 of 5730 years, but not corrected according to the tree-ring chronology, as tree-ring corrections are not available for such an early date: see Glossary).

These first Knossians of the seventh millennium were already using obsidian from Melos, but apparently did not have pottery even though they knew how to fire clay, as their buildings are partly made of fired mud brick. We must imagine that they used baskets or skins for containers. They were farming people and their settlement probably became quite large, as much as about 2 hectares or 5 acres spread over the original hillock. Children's burials were found in level X around the houses, including both newly-born children and a foetus.

The Early Neolithic I culture of these people – to give them their archaeological label – continued till level V which is dated by Carbon-14 to 5260 ± 180. The word 'culture' is a technical term in archaeology for 'a constantly recurring assemblage of artefacts' (Gordon Childe in 1929), which one hopes indicates a homogeneous group of people: problems arise, of course, when the culture changes, when one must decide how much a change in the material evidence reflects a change in the group of people who made the culture. At Knossos there was such a change in level VII, when building in mud bricks gave way to building in packed mud or *pisé* laid on a foundation of stones and *kouskouras*, the soft, white local limestone marl. The excavator judged that this was only a change within the culture of Early Neolithic I and was not significant enough to merit the title of a new culture.

Where the Early Neolithic I people came from is not certain, but their closest links may be with North-West Asia Minor. The period was followed by Early Neolithic II (level IV) and Middle and Late Neolithic (levels III–I): the first metal implement in Crete, a copper axehead, was found in a Late Neolithic level. Besides Knossos, there were other Late Neolithic settlements at Phaistos and elsewhere in Crete.

If we know little about how the Neolithic peoples arrived in Crete, we know equally little about how they left, or came to an end, and were then succeeded by the Minoans. Perhaps there was a gap in Crete's history and the Minoans arrived at deserted sites? Or Neolithic survivors may have mixed with Minoan immigrants? Or perhaps there were no Minoan immigrants at all, but rather the Early Minoan culture grew out of the Neolithic in a way that is not yet clear? We cannot tell. New excavations are being made to try and solve these problems. They are important ones since the central problem behind them is one of great interest: who in fact were the Minoans?

After the four and a half millennia of Neolithic culture the Minoan era lasted for about two millennia, from about 3000 to close to 1000 B.C. It was called Minoan by Sir Arthur Evans, after Minos the legendary king of Knossos, when Evans invented the 'Minoan' system to be a framework for the changes in stratification and the associated developments in styles of pottery that he found in excavating the palace at Knossos.

Minoan Chronology

The Minoan system is divided into Early, Middle and Late periods (on the analogy of the Old, Middle and New Kingdoms of Egypt), which are divided in turn into three phases, some of which have been subdivided into A and B, and some of these even further into 1 and 2. Cretan archaeologists thus talk of Early Minoan II, or E.M.II, which is about 2600–2200 B.C., or of Late Minoan IIIA1 (L.M.IIIA1), which is from a little before 1400 to about 1375 B.C. This notation is used to refer simultaneously to style and to period, in the same way as a phrase like 'Queen Anne' can both describe and date a piece of furniture; and, as with antique furniture, it is not easy always to distinguish the two uses. The distinctions are not a problem at Knossos as the system was invented there, but they can be difficult in the rest of the island where styles may begin earlier or later in the provinces than in the centre, or be different or even not occur at all. So Early Minoan III in East Crete, with pottery characteristically decorated in creamy-white curves and spirals continued after Knossos had changed from its Early Minoan III to the polychrome style of Middle Minoan IA painted in red and white on a black ground. Later, Middle Minoan II pottery (Plate 4) was a sophisticated court style confined only to Knossos, Phaistos and Mallia, while the rest of the island still continued in a Middle Minoan IB style. Likewise in Late Minoan times the fine vases of Late Minoan IB and II may have been made at Knossos alone. These overlappings are indicated by diagonal lines in the chronological table (Fig. 3).

A different sort of problem arising from Evans's system has been that his periods do not concur with the major stages of the architectural history of the palaces. So the first palaces, on Evans's system, were begun in Middle Minoan

IB, and their replacements in Middle Minoan III. These divergences have led Professor Platon to propose his 'palatial' system of Minoan chronology. He has divided the Minoan era into Prepalatial (Early Minoan and probably Middle Minoan IA), Protopalatial (Middle Minoan I and II, ended by the destruction of the Old Palaces), Neopalatial (Middle Minoan III to Late Minoan IB and IIIA1, ended by the different destructions of the New Palaces), and Postpalatial (the rest of Late Minoan III). His system in general reflects more faithfully what happened, but is not so fine as Evans's: a shortcoming, for instance, is that it does not easily distinguish between the destructions of the country houses and of all the New Palaces except Knossos around 1450 (Late Minoan IB) and that of Knossos some 75 years later (Late Minoan IIIA1/2). I shall take a middle course in this book and refer to the Old and New Palaces, and to the periods before and after them, but always within the framework of Evans.

The Minoan system provides the relative chronology of Crete in the Bronze Age. That is to say, it is used to relate one Minoan object to another in sequence, but it cannot provide the absolute dates in years B.C. They can be found mostly from Crete's contacts with Egypt and the East, as there are few Carbon-14 dates yet available for Crete, while in Egypt a fairly well-dated history exists going back to the beginning of the third millenium. The contacts consist of the Minoan objects found in the East Mediterranean together with dated local finds and the Egyptian and Near Eastern objects found in similar situations in Crete. Of course, there are difficulties. Either the objects or their foreign find spots may not be securely dateable in themselves; and it is not easy to tell how many years elapsed between the objects' being made and their being deposited. Sometimes there are no foreign objects that can be used as links. One can then rely only on stylistic or technical parallels between different areas or, as a last resort, assign an arbitrary number of years to fit into a gap. The Early Minoan period is dated in this secondary way. Early Minoan II jewellery seems similar to that from the Royal Cemetery at Ur in Mesopotamia of the second half of the third millennium and there are links with Early Helladic II of the Greek mainland, and Early Minoan III stoneware may imitate some Egyptian shapes of the centuries before the Middle Kingdom, which began in 1991 B.C. This allows then:

Early Minoan III	c.2200–2050 (its terminal date being governed by the succeeding Middle Minoan IA),
Early Minoan II	c.2600–2200, and finally
Early Minoan I	c.3000–2600,

being taken back to the beginning of the third millennium, to coincide with the Egyptian First Dynasty. Early Minoan I seems to have been a long period, to judge by the (slow) development of its pottery.

Imported finished products are not known in Crete for certain till the Middle Minoan period. About twenty scarab seals have been found in Middle Minoan I and II deposits, which date the beginning of the period to just before 2000. About the same time Middle Minoan II pottery was exported to the East but little of it is in well-dated contexts there.

Middle Minoan II was ended by earthquakes which destroyed the Old

Palaces. The succeeding phase, Middle Minoan III, saw the rebuilding of the palaces, much as we have them now, though other earthquakes interrupted the work. In the first subphase, M.M.IIIA, there is at last an indisputable synchronism at Knossos which can survive sceptical scrutiny. The lid of a stone vase with the cartouche of the pharoah Khyan (second half of the seventeenth century) was found with M.M.IIIA pottery; and pottery of the second sub-phase, M.M. IIIB, has affinities and is probably contemporary with that of the last phase of the Middle Bronze Age of Palestine and Syria, which ended about 1550 B.C.

In the Late Minoan period we have three certain synchronisms on which to hang the rest of the chronology. The first is that Minoan objects known particularly in Late Minoan IB are shown painted in the tombs of high officials of the pharoah Thothmosis III (1504–1450); the second is that the Late Minoan IIIA1 subphase is approximately contemporary with the reign of Amenophis III (1417–1379); and finally some Late Minoan IIIA2 wares are contemporary with Late Helladic IIIA2, vases of which have been found in the city of the pharoah Akhenaten at el Amarna, which was occupied only from about 1365 to 1350. We insert among these dates two most important events in Minoan history, the destruction of most of the palaces and country houses at the end of the Late Minoan IB period and the destruction of Knossos at a time when the Late Minoan IIIA1 style was changing to that of Late Minoan IIIA2. Late Minoan IB lasted then roughly as long as the reign of Thothmosis III, say 1500–1450, and so Late Minoan IA can be fitted into 1550–1500. The first destructions happened around 1450. Late Minoan II lasted from 1450 to about 1400, and Late Minoan IIIA1, which must be contemporary with Amenophis III, from about 1400 to about 1375. Knossos was destroyed say about 1375 at the transition from Late Minoan IIIA1 to IIIA2. The remaining Late Minoan phases can be dated only by their parallels with the Late Helladic phases of mainland Greece. So Late Minoan IIIA2 lasted from about 1375 to 1300, IIIB from 1300 to 1200, and IIIC from 1200 till close to 1000. In their final centuries, as in the Early Minoan period, the Minoans had no palaces. We shall now turn to this Early Minoan period; but first you may find it easier to understand Minoan chronology and its difficulties – which have to be the basis of any historical account of the Minoans – if you consult the chronological table. On it are shown the absolute dates, and the Minoan era divided both according to Evans's system and according to the 'palatial' system, with the major events indicated by the appropriate arch-aeological phase and other relevant contemporary events in the East Mediterr-anean included to show Crete in her international setting (Fig. 3).

Before the Palaces

The earliest Minoan phase, Early Minoan I (3000–2600), is obscure. Settlements have been found at Knossos and Phaistos and at a number of places beside the sea on the North coast. This might mean that immigrants came from abroad and set up camp by the sea, or sometimes settled in caves near where they landed – only later to penetrate inland – but one would expect also that some of the previous Neolithic inhabitants survived. Early Minoan I pottery was made by

Fig. 3. Chronological Table

B.C.	Egypt		Crete	Aegean
3100	Dynasty	Early Minoan		
3000	I			
2900				
2800	II	I		
2700				
	III			
2600	IV			
2500	User Kaf			
	V	II	*Floruit* of Vasiliki and Fournou Korifi	Minoan settlement on Kythera
2400				
2300	VI			
2200	VII–X	III		
2100	XI			
2000		Middle Minoan 1A		
1900	XII	1B	OLD PALACES	
1800	XIII and Hyksos	IIA		
1700				
	Khyan	IIB		
1600		IIIA	Country houses begun	Minoan expansion in South Aegean begins
		IIIB	NEW PALACES	
1500	XVIII Hatshepsut Thothmosis III (1504-1450)	Late Minoan 1A		Eruption of Thera
		1B	Destruction of most palaces and country houses	Decline of Minoan influence in South Aegean
1400	Amenophis III (1417-1379)	II	Destruction of Knossos	
		IIIA1		
		IIIA2	Khania capital?	Burst of Mycenaean exporting to East Mediterranean
1300	XIX	IIIB		
1200	XX	IIIC	Immigrants from mainland Greece	Destruction of Mycenaean centres
1100		(and ? Sub-Minoan)		
1000	XXI			
900	XXII	Protogeometric		

hand: typical products are a smoky black ware with patterns burnished on the surface – similar vases in Samos might indicate that some, at least, of the Early Minoan I people came from Asia Minor. There was also a painted ware, often used for jugs, with red and brown lines on a white surface, sometimes in the reverse technique. The use of paint on pottery at this period has no parallels nearer than South-East Turkey or even Palestine, from where other immigrants could also have come to Crete. It is interesting that the counterpoint of dark-on-light and light-on-dark in pottery decoration had already begun in Early Minoan I: the play of the two styles is characteristic of all the two thousand years of Minoan pottery. Sometimes one predominates and sometimes the other.

We hardly know what Early Minoan I houses were like, but a well of this phase at Knossos, dug 17.20 m. deep, is evidence of their engineering skill. They often buried their dead in rock shelters and caves, but they also began to build circular communal tombs, a habit which lasted into Middle Minoan times. These tombs are built of corbelled stones laid with a pronounced inward batter, as the Mycenaean *tholos* tombs of mainland Greece were later, and they may have been roofed with a continuous stone vault, like the Mycenaean ones,

2   The Goddess of Myrtos (from Fournou Korifi) holds a jug which is a miniature of a type of Early Minoan II. The Goddess herself is a pouring vase: the spout of the miniature is the actual spout. Perhaps she was the patron of a group of potters at Fournou Korifi making these striped jugs, or perhaps she protected the water supply.

or perhaps with wattle and daub on a timber framework. Since the Cretan circular tombs are preserved only to a few metres' height one cannot be certain either way. Some of the tombs were cut into hillsides and so could have been more easily vaulted, while others standing free on open ground are more suited for a frame roof with wattle and daub. The largest tomb, tomb A at Platanos some 12 km. away from Phaistos in the Mesara plain, is on open flat ground and has an internal diameter of 13.10 m. – to roof that with stone would surely have been beyond the powers of its Early Minoan builders. It must have had something lighter. Once built, these tombs were used by villages, or by families or clans (extended families), for centuries. Old burials and the offerings with them were pushed aside to make room for the new corpse or, when the flesh had rotted, the bones were put into bone-chambers which were annexes outside the entrance. The entrance was always low so that even the Minoans had to stoop. As far as we know, they were small people, the men about 1.60 to 1.70 m. high. The women were a little shorter.

Early Minoan II (2600–2200) developed out of Early Minoan I and produced a surprisingly sophisticated culture. New techniques appeared, such as making stone vases, making faience and cutting seals in stone and ivory. Some of these ideas may have come from the older civilisations of the East, as the ivory certainly did. The seals, for instance, are important not just for being the first Minoan seals made but because they show also that there was already in Early Minoan II a developed sense of property. Clay sealings have been found, pieces of clay put over the mouth of a jar and stamped with a seal to prevent anyone's robbing the contents. This picture of growth and prosperity is reflected in the

3   A pyramidal seal in steatite (soapstone) from the settlement at Pyrgos near Myrtos. It can be worn on a string round the neck, and has a simple linear design. Similar seals from Fournou Korifi date this chance find to Early Minoan II.

4 The Palm Jar from Knossos of Middle Minoan II B (1700–1625: end of the Old Palaces). The half seen here is in the Ashmolean Museum, and the other in the Heraklion Museum. The decoration is becoming stiffer and is placed in a more open field. The palm tree may have been introduced to Crete from the Near East at about this time.

quality of the buildings at Vasiliki and Fournou Korifi, which are the best known E.M.II settlements and are both in East Crete. Fournou Korifi near the present village of Myrtos is a complex of about eighty rooms joined to each other. What sort of society was living there? Since it is all one building, an extended family perhaps formed the village. Besides pottery and stone implements, it has produced sealstones (cf. Plate 3) and figurines (a remarkable figurine vase – Plate 2) and some well made buildings. Vasiliki has been less excavated, but what may be one of the first grand Minoan houses has been found there, with red wall plaster still on the walls and a courtyard on the West side of the building which may anticipate the West courts of the later palaces. Vasiliki has given its name to a distinctive pottery of the later part of Early Minoan II, Vasiliki ware, which is mottled red to black, with a polished surface and with rounded and sometimes extravagant shapes. Typical is the 'teapot'. The mottling was probably achieved by placing coals nearer or farther from the pot in the firing, thus making more oxidisation (black) or less (red). Another great house of Early Minoan II has been uncovered recently below the West Court of Knossos, which may well be a predecessor to the Middle Minoan palace.

Fig. 4. Map of Crete.

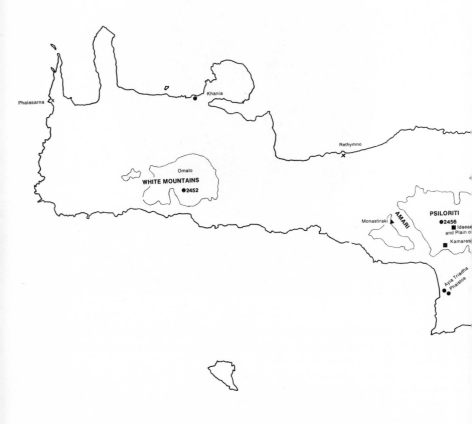

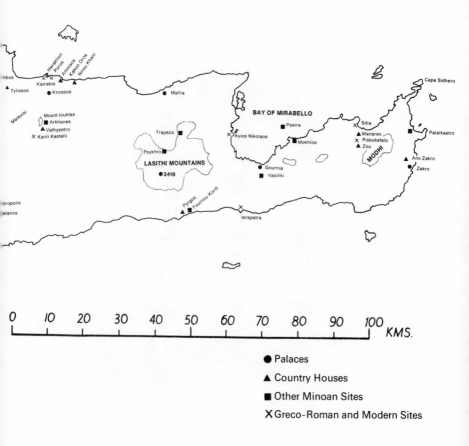

0   10   20   30   40   50   60   70   80   90   100 KMS.

● Palaces
▲ Country Houses
■ Other Minoan Sites
✕ Greco-Roman and Modern Sites

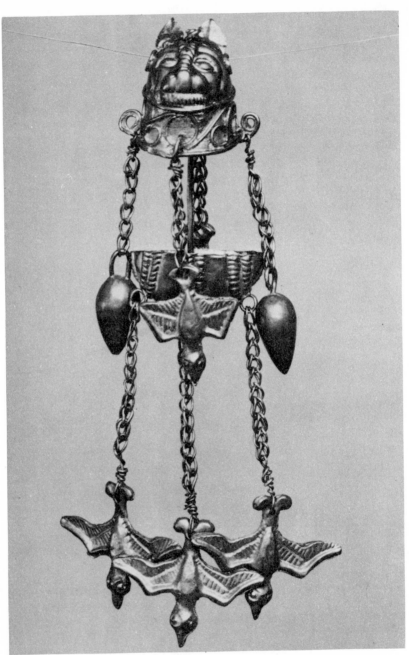

5   Earring pendant of a lion's head with flying ducks. It is part of the so-called 'Aegina Treasure' in the British Museum, which probably comes from the Khrysolakkos cemetery at Mallia.

Possibly the most striking creation of all that the Early Minoan II culture achieved is the jewellery from the tombs of Mokhlos, a seaport not far from Vasiliki. There gold diadems, hairpins of crocus flowers and leaves, pendants and other costume jewellery have been found. They are elegant and natural, and as attractive as such later Minoan jewellery as the 'Aegina Treasure' (Plate 5). Several other gold treasures of much the same date have been found in Asia Minor and around the Aegean, which suggests that the arrival of prosperity in Early Minoan II was not a phenomenon confined to Crete but was something more widespread.

Besides prospering at home, the Minoans expanded abroad to the small island of Kythera which is between the North-West point of Crete and the South-East tip of the Peloponnese. Here a settlement was founded at Kastri, with pottery so similar to that of West Crete around Khania that the settlers of Kastri must have come from that region. This first Minoan colony was set on a small promontory with beaches on either side, and fertile and well watered valleys behind. It is virtually the ideal spot for a settlement, as had already been noticed by Early Helladic people who were occupying a knoll 100 m. away from the Minoan site. Their occupation ended, however, in Early Helladic II, perhaps because they left of their own accord, or perhaps because the Minoans pushed them out. The discovery of a Minoan settlement outside Crete as early as Early Minoan II came as a surprise, as nobody had expected developments abroad so early. Another surprise from Kythera is a tiny stone vase inscribed with the name of the Sun-Temple of the pharoah User Kaf, the first king of the Egyptian Fifth Dynasty which began in c.2494. Although it is impossible to tell exactly how this vase reached Kythera, it is likely that Minoans brought it. If they did, its date is appropriate to the founding of Crete's first colony in Early Minoan II.

Early Minoan II was ended at Vasiliki and Fournou Korifi by fires, fierce destructions that remind us of those that destroyed so many of the Cretan centres in 1450. We do not know if this E.M. II destruction was as general as the fifteenth-century one, since so few E.M. II settlements have been excavated. It may have been the work of enemies, or of pirates (as there are similar destructions at many other centres in the Aegean), or of earthquakes which tipped over lighted lamps.

The succeeding phase, Early Minoan III (2200–2050) has characteristics that differ in Knossos and the centre of Crete from those in the East. At Knossos it was probably a short phase, anticipating the longer Middle Minoan IA. Its pottery has white line decoration on a red or black ground, and during Middle Minoan IA spirals were adopted as a decorative motif. The different development in East Crete – which might tell us something of events at the end of Early Minoan II, if our knowledge were not so sketchy – was to more curving shapes of vase than in the centre of the island, with decoration in creamy-white paint, making curving and running patterns. This style continued for a while after the centre had moved on to polychrome Middle Minoan IA (the evidence is imports and exports of the two styles found in the centre and in the East of Crete), but thereafter the East followed the centre in adopting the polychrome tradition.

There are few house remains of Early Minoan III, but some of Middle

Minoan IA can be seen at the bottom of large circular pits known as *koulouras* in the West Court of Knossos (Fig. 6.2). Several of the houses' fittings are built of, and covered in, red plaster, and the floors also are of plaster. The effect would have been like that of wall-to-wall carpeting, continued right up the walls.

Another find from Knossos of Middle Minoan IA date is a hoard of sacred offerings, the Vat Room deposit (Fig. 6.26), which was covered when the palace was built. It is in the room next to a later hoard of sacred offerings, the so-called Temple Repositories (Fig. 6.24) and, as Evans remarked, taken together they may be evidence that this particular area was sacred for over half a millennium. The Vat Room deposit contained Middle Minoan IA pottery, pieces of stone vases, faience and gold foil, and the shell of an ostrich egg.

Crafts continued to develop in Early Minoan III and Middle Minoan IA and were stimulated by more contacts with abroad. Some stone vases may be copies from contemporary Egyptian shapes, and the coppersmiths adopted improvements from their colleagues in Byblos. In fact some Byblite daggers were imported into Crete, and Byblite and Minoan daggers have both been found in Cyprus where traders from both sides could have met coming for the same purpose of acquiring some of that island's abundant copper. A Middle Minoan IA jar has been found in Cyprus, and small stone vases have turned up in Gezer in Palestine, and in Euboia, Samos and the Argolid. Cretan pottery went to the settlement of Lerna in the Argolid (where it includes East Cretan Early Minoan III as well as Knossian Middle Minoan IA) and to Phylakopi, the chief Bronze Age town on the obsidian island of Melos. In return, the Cyclades may have passed on to Crete the motif of the spiral, which remained in the Minoan artistic repertoire till the end of their civilisation.

These new skills, the closer contacts with abroad and the greater sophistication of the Minoans are the prelude to one of the most momentous events in their story, the founding of the palaces. In the next chapter we shall look at the first palaces and discover more of the needs, pressures and effects of this industrial development which occurred around the beginning of the second millennium, and how it was that the palaces came into being then. It is a fascinating story of the political, social, economic and cultural effects of a new technology, which resulted in what we call Europe's first civilisation.

2 The Old Palaces

The first Minoan palaces were built in Middle Minoan IB (1900–1800) and were destroyed at the end of Middle Minoan IIB (1700–1625). These three centuries saw, besides the foundation of the palaces, remarkable technical advances, more regular contacts with the Levant, the adoption of a script for writing, and the first flowering of Minoan art into a formal, but lively, style. The period of the Old Palaces was the first of two classical periods of Minoan civilisation. We can still recognise an authority and a zest, even though little is left now except pottery and a few buildings, which define together the archaeology of the period. Its earlier part, Middle Minoan IB, has the characteristics of an archaic phase preceding a classical Middle Minoan II. Middle Minoan II is a sophisticated style that apparently was confined to the courts of Knossos, Phaistos and Mallia. Elsewhere in the island Middle Minoan IB continued little changed, ending at about the same time as did the Middle Minoan IIB style of the palaces, when the whole of Crete may have been concussed by earthquakes. Such a contrast between sophistication and provincial simplicity was not known in the Early Minoan period: one must see it as a consequence of the foundation of the palaces. It is the best evidence left to us of the importance they immediately assumed.

At the same time as they began to build the palaces, the Minoans also started to use the free-moving potter's wheel, one of the most important technical advances in their history: we do not know how the idea arose. The potter's wheel enabled them to produce lighter vases in greater numbers. Shapes became both more fluid and more defined, so that angles were sharper and curves more sinuous than when pots had been made by hand by the coil method or on a simple disc that could be pushed around in the earth. Another important advance in potting followed a little later, the discovery of how to make very thin-walled vases. Some of these vases are so thin that they are known as 'eggshell ware': they are well fired, hard and brittle, and the sherds give a fine clink if dropped. They are too thin to have been made on the wheel, and were probably made in moulds, but the clay would have had to be very carefully sifted to prevent cracking when the vase dried in the mould and when it was fired.

Eggshell ware is the most distinctive of all Minoan pottery, because of its fine fabric, elegant shapes, and flowing formal decoration in red and white on a black ground. The most common shape in eggshell ware is a hemispherical cup about the size of half a grapefruit or slightly larger, with a sharply everted rim. It may have a central boss at the bottom. This boss, the thinness of the walls, the resemblance of the shape to a contemporary silver cup at Byblos, and the high black gloss which often turned the colour of bronze in the firing all suggest that the Minoan potters were trying to recreate in their clay eggshell ware a shape of vase which already existed in metal. Thereafter the hemispherical cup became very popular in pottery, continuing to be made until after the time of the fall of Knossos in the early fourteenth century.

Another type of vase to appear after the discovery of the potter's wheel is the Vafio cup (cf. Plate 6), a flat-based cup of the shape of an inverted truncated cone: this shape had an equally long life and may be similarly one which metalworkers had discovered first. Plenty of later parallels in silver and gold are known, the most famous of them the two gold cups with relief bulls and cows of Late Minoan IB style from the tomb at Vafio near Sparta which gave its name to that shape. Besides these cups, another popular Minoan vase which, though known since Early Minoan II, became established in the repertoire only in the time of the Old Palaces was the bridge-spouted jar. It is a vase with inturned shoulder, two handles on the sides and a spout starting from below the rim under a 'bridge' so that it could pour more easily. Two other new types confirm how sensitive the Minoan potters were to what was being made in other materials: a flask which imitates leather flasks or bottles, and an oval rhyton (a vase with a wide hole at the top and a small one at the bottom used for pouring liquids in ritual) which copies the shape of ostrich eggs. Ostrich eggs with holes drilled in them were already used in this way in ceremonies and rituals.

The decoration of pottery developed with the new shapes. In Middle Minoan IB the motifs were more curved than before, but they were still rather stiff and

6 Late Minoan IA (1550–1500) Vafio cup from Knossos. The Vafio shape had been made from the time of the introduction of the potter's wheel in Middle Minoan IB. Spirals are a common design on Late Minoan IA vases.

angular, except for some exotic polychrome imitations of the veinings of the stone of stone vases – the effect is like that of a painting by Jackson Pollock. In the peak period of eggshell ware, Middle Minoan IIA, spirals, curves, trefoils, pendants and other formalised plant designs flowed over the vases with a zest and ease that makes them a delight to look at and a pleasure to handle. This style of pottery, often known as Kamares ware after the cave of Kamares near Phaistos where it was first noticed at the end of the last century, is of an astounding sophistication, but it did not last for long: it began to ossify in the final years of life of the Old Palaces, Middle Minoan IIB, but even vases of that period are impressive both in themselves (Plate 4) and when contrasted with the provincial wares of the rest of the island. This Kamares pottery was popular abroad, as we shall see: it was the finest pottery of its time in the whole East Mediterranean.

We shall now turn from the pottery of the Old Palaces to the buildings which are the other prime constituent of the archaeological record of the period. Unfortunately, the building history is difficult to make out since, when the New Palaces were begun, there was immediate rebuilding (in Middle Minoan III) on the ruins of the Old Palaces. You will see most surviving of one of the Old Palaces at Phaistos; there is only a little visible at Knossos and Mallia, though an important building of the period is being uncovered at Mallia at some distance from the palace.

At Phaistos so much of the Old Palace has been preserved mainly because its South-West quarter was hardly built on in New Palace time, while the West facade of the New Palace was set 5 m. in from the facade of the Old Palace and a metre above the former ground level (Plate 24). This has left several rooms and storerooms, the West facade itself, an elaborate West entrance and the West Court of the Old Palace all preserved, and in the South-West quarter a complex of rooms standing fairly intact up to two or three storeys built against the edge of the hill. Perhaps a reason why this area was not incorporated in the New Palace was that it was thought to be in an unstable situation on the edge of the hill.

The Old Palace at Mallia could have been similar to the present New Palace, a simple building; but very little is preserved. It is possible that the important building (Area Mu) being excavated nearby may have been used for some of the purposes that the palaces were used for elsewhere. At Knossos the West Court was not constructed until Middle Minoan II, at which time circular pits were left in the Court (Fig. 6.2). There are similar pits of the Old Palace period at Phaistos (Plate 24), and at Mallia (Plate 32), where they are continued above ground level. They may all have been granaries.

It has been thought that the palaces were originally divided into separate blocks, reflecting a development from buildings grouped around a village square; but it is far from certain that this view is correct. The village square may very likely be the progenitor of the Central Court, but the palaces we see built around them appear to be single units which have overcome the limitations of houses round a square. However, the rounded North-East corner of the Throne Room block (Fig. 6.17) at Knossos has often been thought part of an originally separate building in the Old Palace. Other Old Palace remains at Knossos are the pottery stores at the North-East corner and the so-called 'Keep' at the North end of the Central Court (Fig. 6.13) whose steep and sheer walls remind one of Norman architecture. Contrary to what one would expect the Keep was not a military stronghold; rather, it served to hold up the North part of the Palace on the edge of the hill – its walls are like piles – and perhaps was also used for storing grain in its large cavities. To imagine the Old Palace at Knossos, one must see it as being on much more of a hill than one sees now, with the ground sloping away on the West as well as on the East.

We have some idea of private dwellings of the time, as a collection of faience plaques representing houses was found at Knossos in a level of rubbish belonging to the first phase of the New Palace period, Middle Minoan IIIA. The plaques were probably made in the time of the Old Palaces, and were either inlays in a picture or were movable and could be arranged to make one's own picture, perhaps as a game for children. The beams are shown in section as well as lengthways; and there are windows, some of which have vertical divisions and even sashes and doors. The courses of the blocks are picked out, perhaps to show that the blocks are laid on a bed of clay. This type of construction is like that of timbered Tudor houses; and there are nearer parallels in some of the Turkish houses in Heraklion, Rethymno and Khania in Crete. The use of timbers gives the buildings an elastic strength to survive earthquakes.

Our understanding of the functions of the Old Palaces can only be inferred from what we know of the plans, uses of the rooms and contents of their New Palace counterparts, which are discussed in detail below. From their evidence we shall see that the New Palaces were essential to virtually every aspect of Minoan life, whether religious, political, social, economic or cultural; and there is no reason to doubt that the same holds for the Old Palaces. We shall now examine some of the probable effects of the founding of the Old Palaces.

First, when the palaces were founded in Middle Minoan IB, it must have meant that there was at that time more authoritarian political control or more political cohesion than before, more for instance than would have been needed to build Vasiliki or Fournou Korifi. The building operations would have needed large numbers of men, perhaps levies, who would have had to be fed. The intricacies of control could have been a spur to the adoption of writing.

Second, there was economic growth. The farmers of the island had to be able to yield a surplus sufficient to feed the people working on the palaces, the staff and craftsmen living in them, and probably enough over and above that for the king (if there was a king) to send abroad to exchange for the luxuries and essentials he could not find in Crete. Only by such a reconstruction can one explain the exceptionally large area of the palaces devoted to storage. In these storerooms the corn, wine, oil, currants, wool and cloth were kept to satisfy all these demands. In turn the craftsmen in the palaces would seem to have produced more than was needed or thought appropriate at home, as some of their products were sent abroad. The very fact that most of the Middle Minoan pottery found outside Crete is of the Middle Minoan II style, which as we saw is confined to the palaces, shows that foreign trade was controlled by the palaces. With the economic development of the Old Palace period the population of Crete would have grown as well.

In the arts and crafts, the rulers of the palaces would have been the patrons. They doubtless gathered craftsmen around their courts, and could give them the stimulus of new techniques learnt from their foreign contacts. Many of the finest products were stored in treasuries attached to the palace shrines – evidence again of the surplus in production that Crete enjoyed.

What effect the founding of the palaces had on religious practice is difficult to say. Presumably the idea that the palaces were sacred buildings – a belief which pervades the New Palaces – grew up in the time of the Old Palaces and was probably fostered by the rulers. Religion was a powerful force to ensure loyalty; and if the founding of the palaces really did lead to a better life in Crete, then it is quite possible that before long the rulers were thought to be divine. It is almost certain that they were thought so at the time of the New Palaces, and it would be surprising if this did not hold equally for the earlier period.

Finally, there is the remarkable fact that no defence walls have been discovered around the Old Palaces and their towns, nor around the New Palaces (except possibly one at Mallia of Middle Minoan III date). By contrast with the Cyclades and mainland Greece where fortifications were relatively common at this time, palatial Crete seems to have had peace at home and no fear of invasion from abroad – a quite astonishing state of affairs, in which wealth and the population would have grown. One effect would have been that the palaces became all the more important.

Such then may have been the effects of the founding of the palaces. What we cannot tell is how the idea of them may have actually arisen. There are plenty of similarities in their functions with the palaces of the Near East, though the amount of space devoted to the storage of farm produce is more than one finds there, and their style of architecture does not have parallels abroad. The palaces were founded probably as a response to the pressures of the industrial development at the end of the Early Bronze Age and, like the industrial techniques, they were affected by the Near Eastern experience – although there is nothing one can point to in the palaces as being specifically Near Eastern. We shall now look at something of the bureaucracy, trade, and arts of the Old Palaces, the practical effects of their founding, and end with a discussion of the burial customs and religion of the period.

The appearance of writing during the life of the Old Palaces was an important development for the future of the Minoan civilisation. Its immediate effect was to produce a bureaucracy – bureaucracy begins by distinguishing those who know how to write and ends by giving them power over those who do not. The first script of this bureaucracy was called 'Hieroglyphic' by Evans. The Hieroglyphic texts are found either on seals or seal impressions with a few signs or clay tablets and labels. All three of the Old Palaces have yielded texts, but there are very few of them. We do not have enough to know the language. Like Linear A and Linear B, it was probably syllabic; and the choice of its signs may have been influenced by the hieroglyphic writing of Egypt, after which Evans named the Minoan Hieroglyphic. At least, the script does show that the palaces had both a regular system for writing things down, probably in lists and tax documents as we know the Linear B tablets were, and a more sophisticated way of marking possessions, by the texts on the seals. Apart from the use of a syllabary, the script has two features which continued into Linear A and Linear B: one is a system of standard ideograms, or picture-signs, so that the illiterate could recognise what was the subject of the text: the other is a decimal system of numbering. The demands of administering the palaces produced these systems and the Hieroglyphic script.

Trade with the Levant grew with the impetus of the founding of the palaces, and with the new stability created in the Levant by the control of the Egyptian Twelfth Dynasty after a period of troubles. Imports into Crete were probably still mainly raw materials essential for the quality of palatial life, whether copper or ivory, or spices; but some small finished luxury products came, such as Egyptian scarabs and Babylonian cylinder seals. In Kythera the lid of a box for keeping such cylinders was found in the last century, and at Knossos there have been two surprises from Egypt, a flint knife and the statuette of an Egyptian private citizen, who could even have come to Knossos and left it behind as a visiting card. In turn Cretan pots went to Cyprus, Syria and Egypt, one travelling as far inland as Qatna in the Orontes valley (map, Fig. 1). They are rather more frequent in the great cities on the Syrian coast of Ras Shamra and Byblos. In Egypt a bridge-spouted jar was taken far up the Nile to Abydos. These examples of Old Palace pottery found abroad are some of the best preserved pieces we have and are of the typical and distinctive Minoan shapes that have been described, the bridge-spouted jar and the hemispherical and Vafio cups. The jar shape was unusual enough to be copied by local potters in Syria and in Egypt.

Besides pottery, Crete may also have exported metalware. Some silver cups found in a foundation deposit in a temple at Tod in Upper Egypt which are definitely not Egyptian have often been thought to be Minoan. In fact they are not at all like the one silver cup of the period known from Crete nor do they have many of the traits of Minoan pottery which one can reasonably think to be derived from metalworking. At Byblos however some silver and bronze cups are more likely to be Minoan products: they are of the Minoan hemispherical shape – which was not known by other East Mediterranean potters – and one has a *repoussé* decoration of dots and spirals, which are motifs one often finds painted on Cretan clay cups of this shape.

Byblos may have been particularly important to the Minoans at this time: we have seen already that she could have taught Crete some improvements in copper- and bronzesmithery, and she (or Ras Shamra) may also have supplied Crete with tin from places further East. Another trick which Crete could have learnt from Byblos was granulation in gold work, the art of making small grains of gold and fixing them onto a piece of jewellery. This art appeared in Byblos about a century before it did in Crete. Two other techniques which began in Crete about the time the palaces were founded could also be derived from Byblos: the potter's wheel, and the use of a tubular drill to hollow out the insides of stone vases, and to make concentric circles on sealstones. In view then of Crete's commercial and technical links with Byblos, one might even wonder whether her trade with Egypt was not conducted by way of Byblos and that Minoans in fact hardly or never travelled up the Nile. Egypt had had very strong trade ties with Byblos for centuries, since Byblos controlled and exported the cedars of Lebanon which the Egyptians needed continually. Something else Byblos may have sent Crete at this time was the date palm, which is shown for the first time in Crete on a Middle Minoan IIB jar from Knossos (Plate 4). With the possible arrival of the palm we shall leave the foreign trade of the Old Palaces.

Unfortunately, we have little evidence for the arts of the Old Palaces apart from pottery. You realise this when you see how few non-ceramic finds there are in the Old Palace rooms in the Heraklion Museum and how many in the New Palace rooms. One art which was probably practised in the palaces is fresco painting; but no Old Palace frescoes survive. New Palace frescoes are described in the next chapter.

Sealstones are the objects best known after pottery. Many have survived. A workshop for them has been found at Mallia, and at Phaistos a hoard of some seven thousand clay sealings was found, from which we can learn the designs of a very large number of seals. Surprisingly, the fluid and yet crisp elegance of the vases is only occasionally found in the designs on the sealstones. Although these designs are, as on the vases, mostly formal, they are curiously static – perhaps because of the restricted working area. The new technique of the tubular drill allowed more depth than before; and a few animals and stylised humans were introduced and were more common than on vases.

Jewellery became more interesting with the new processes such as granulation. An example of this is a toad with its warts – although it is possibly a lion with its mane – from a communal tomb at Koumasa, an exquisite and lively piece. The largest collection of jewellery is the so-called Aegina Treasure (in the British Museum), which probably does not come from Aegina but from the Khrysolakkos ('Gold Pit') cemetery near Mallia; if this is so, a companion to the Treasure is the famous pendant of two wasps or bees eating a berried fruit, one of the glories of Minoan art which is on display in the Heraklion Museum. The pieces in the British Museum are less well known but quite as interesting. Among the best of them is the Master of the Animals, a man holding two geese and standing perhaps in a marsh with lotuses, with what are sun disks below, and the pendant of a lion's head earring (Plate 5) with flying ducks. The Master of the Animals is rarer in Minoan iconography than the Mistress, of which the faience goddesses from Knossos holding snakes are the best known examples. The naturalism in this jewellery was in the forefront of a trend that can be seen occasionally in the designs of sealstones and vases. It became more marked in the period of the New Palaces. In fact, as far as the Aegina Treasure and the Khrysolakkos pieces are concerned, one cannot say for sure whether they all or in part belong to Middle Minoan IIB and the end of the Old Palaces, or to Middle Minoan III and the first phase of the New Palaces; but these distinctions are unimportant since they are examples of the finest work of the style of the time around the end of the Old Palaces. This style did not change overnight when the palaces were destroyed and the Middle Minoan IIB of the archaeologists was replaced by Middle Minoan IIIA.

We shall end our account of the Old Palaces with a look at burial customs and religion. Old habits of burial continued unchanged during the period of the Old Palaces and the communal built tombs and caves were still used by the Minoans.

As the period went on, the built tombs began to be replaced by large pits dug for communal burials, and by building complexes such as Khrysolakkos by Mallia and Fourni near Arkhanes. Khrysolakkos is a rectangular building measuring 39 × 30 m., which is criss-crossed inside by walls to make a large number of small areas: each family may have been entitled to an area. On the East side is a verandah to give shade to those visiting the cemetery, and there is also a room which was probably a small chapel of the dead.

The idea of these complexes may have developed from the ossuaries or bone-chambers which were added onto the built circular tombs. At the same time the last of those old style tombs were being constructed at Kamilari near Phaistos and on the hill of Gypsades at Knossos. Other new methods of burial were in large storage jars, or *pithoi*, and in chamber tombs dug in the rock.

Our knowledge of the religion carried on in the Old Palaces is minimal. One can see an Old Palace shrine at Phaistos (p. 95) but little else has survived. Outside the palaces, caves were still centres of worship, and peak sanctuaries were used as well. These mountain shrines sometimes incorporated caves, and were sometimes built up. They were always visible from afar, and each Minoan centre seems to have had its peak sanctuary on a prominent hill nearby. The sanctuary on Mount Iouktas, the dark, conical hill 7 km. South from Knossos, is an example and, seen from Phaistos and Ayia Triadha, the cave of Kamares on Psiloriti is another. In the plain of Lasithi above the village of Psykhro there is another cave that began to be used in Middle Minoan II: its cult then continued through into the first millennium. This cave may have superseded a cave called Trapeza on the opposite side of the plain which had been in use from Early Minoan I, if not before. Nothing is known from Trapeza after Middle Minoan III. Both these caves have produced Egyptian scarabs, which may be an indication that they were quite important, even though they were a steep climb and several hours away from the nearest palace at Mallia.

3 The New Palaces

The earthquakes that may have caused the end of the life of the Old Palaces seem to have stimulated the Minoans to new and yet more strenuous effort. The period of the New Palaces (1625–1375) which Middle Minoan III (1625–1550) inaugurated is marked by the rebuilding of the three Old Palaces and the building of other palaces and of large country houses, by a greatly increased population – to judge from the evidence of the vast number of sites of the period all over Crete – by some remarkable artistic achievements, by an increased trade with Egypt and Syria in the fifteenth century, and by an extension of Minoan influence throughout the South Aegean as far as Messenia in the South-West Peloponnese. In this period the Minoans were the leading power of the region, but at the same time the Mycenaean Greeks of the mainland were steadily growing in strength until they probably overthrew the Minoans. The end of the palatial civilisation of Crete came in two stages: the first was in the mid-fifteenth century (Late Minoan IB) when virtually all the palaces, country houses and towns except probably the palace of Knossos were destroyed; and the second was in about 1375 (Late Minoan IIIA1/2) when the palace of Knossos and the extant grand town houses there were also destroyed. In this last period of two generations' length the rulers of Knossos were people speaking Greek who must have been Mycenaeans. It is likely that they had conquered Crete at the time of the first destructions and then ruled the island from its capital Knossos. Their Greek Linear B script tablets show places under their control throughout the island, from ku-do-ni-ja (Khania) in the western part of Crete to what is probably Sitia in the eastern part.

We shall return to Middle Minoan III and the beginning of the period of the New Palaces. It was a time when Minoan activity outside Crete is almost of more interest than at home. Contacts with the Aegean islands suddenly became much closer, while those with the Levant temporarily fell off. The links were even more marked in the succeeding Late Minoan IA (1550–1500), when Cycladic pottery closely imitated the Minoan styles, stone vases and other Minoan products were imported, and some of the smallest details of Minoan life – the types of clay weights for looms or shapes of lamps and fireboxes – were reproduced. There is evidence of so much cultural transfusion that it is likely that some Minoans had settled abroad, and had political control in the South Aegean.

The process of adopting Minoan sophistication can be seen in three distinct groups of places (Fig. 2). The first is an island on its own, Kythera, where the old colony of Kastri was given a boost, perhaps with new settlers. It was by then about a thousand years old and had been enjoying a fairly quiet life; suddenly it became more important for the Minoans, probably both for its supply of *murex* shells for making purple dye, and because it was strategically placed on the way to the South Peloponnese. The second group consists of the harbour towns of the Cyclades to the North of Crete, most of which had been established as long as Kastri but had their own Cycladic culture. These old towns include Phylakopi on Melos, Ayia Irini on Kea and probably the towns of Paros and Naxos and perhaps Akrotiri on Thera. Here existing ways of life were transformed to a Minoan pattern: the cultural influence of Crete is obvious, and political influence is likely – perhaps a loose control from Crete, perhaps even an empire acquired by conquest. The third group are several settlements to the North-East of Crete, at Trianda on Rhodes, at Miletos and Iasos on the mainland of Asia Minor, and on Kos, Samos and Karpathos. At these places, except in Miletos, there had been no inhabitants for centuries as far as we can tell, and the Minoan foundations seem to be true colonies, as the one in Kythera had been long before. These three groups formed a belt of strong Minoan influence curving around the whole North coast of Crete from its West to its East ends.

Why did the Minoans turn to the Aegean? Three likely reasons are promoting of trade, relief of overpopulation, and defence or a desire to protect interests. There is little immediate evidence to support the idea of trade as, though many Minoan goods were exported, few things have been found in Crete which could possibly have been sent in return: Kea may be an exception to this claim, as the lead weights of Crete and the Minoan world were probably made there or on the coast of Attica under supervision from Kea. However it may be that the Minoans were interested in the islands and in the Peloponnese, not for what these places supplied of their own but because they could send on to Crete copper and tin received by them from Central Europe. As for the other suggestions, relief of overpopulation is plausible enough since Crete was more densely inhabited in this period than at any time until the Roman Empire. Defence may also have been involved – perhaps against pirates who could have used the Cycladic harbours, perhaps against the growing power of the Greek mainland, perhaps even against a threat from Asia Minor.

As with the islands, so with the Greek mainland, Crete's relations changed at the beginning of the period of the New Palaces. A similarly overwhelming Minoan influence civilised the native Middle Helladic traditions, and the mixture of the two cultures produced what we know as the Mycenaean civilisation. The process of transition from Middle Helladic to Mycenaean is most obvious in the Argolid – this was the time of the famous Grave Circles of Mycenae – and in Messenia in the South-West Peloponnese. In both areas plenty of Minoan and Minoan-style objects and habits of life have been noticed, which reflects the importance at that time of these two parts of the Peloponnese. The Argolid must have been controlled by a powerful dynasty resident at Mycenae, who somehow amassed their gold and other riches and employed Minoan craftsmen to work for them or ordered their products from Crete. In Messenia there were families almost as rich, who were possibly even more susceptible to ideas from Crete. How could these kings and princes afford their wealth? And how did they grow so much in power that around the middle of the fifteenth century they probably took Crete?

Much of the answer may well be economic, that the Aegean now began to receive copper and tin from Central Europe. This could have come down the Adriatic. If so, the Mycenaeans may have controlled the Aegean end of the trade, bartering with the Minoans for craftsmen or works of art. Some of this metal may have been brought along the Corinthian Gulf and so to the Argolid, some to Messenia, where there was such a strong Minoan interest. The colony in Kythera lies on the route from Crete to Messenia.

In dealings with countries outside the Aegean Crete's links with Egypt and Syria were not so strong immediately after the fall of the Old Palaces as they had been before: there were still some contacts – a lid with the name of the pharoah Khyan (later seventeenth century) has for instance been found in a Middle Minoan IIIA level at Knossos – but the Egyptian rulers of that time may not have felt so well disposed to the Minoans, being preoccupied with troubles of their own nearer home.

These reduced contacts revived after the Eighteenth Dynasty established itself in Egypt in about 1570 (or 1552). The new rulers set about re-conquering Syria and Palestine and brought to the East Mediterranean a stability which it had not enjoyed since the Twelfth Dynasty, the time which in Crete had been the beginning of the Old Palaces. Crete benefited from the ensuing prosperity, importing again the fine products of the other countries. Egyptian stone vases were received: some were already over a thousand years old (and so perhaps part of an illegal trade in antiquities), while others were of a shape known as the baggy alabastron which the Minoans copied in clay, sending the copies back to Egypt. Ivory still came from Syria and copper from Cyprus: elephant tusks and ingots were found together at Zakro and may have been part of the same shipload which could have been landed at Zakro to be taken by pack animal to Knossos. A little pottery from Syria and Cyprus was received in Crete and in the island settlements. The Cypriot pots, open white bowls, are very different from any Aegean vases and must have had the appeal of the exotic. They are much too shallow to have been used as containers of food all the way from Cyprus. Two little Cypriot jugs have also been found (in Rhodes) which did probably contain a substance, opium: the shape of these juglets imitates the head of the opium poppy. In all, a considerable amount of the sophisticated paraphernalia of the courts of Crete and the Argolid was imported from further East. The Minoans may have acquired these goods themselves in return for taking abroad their farm produce and pottery. On the other hand it is possible that Easterners came to the Aegean. They certainly had some knowledge of its geography, as a list has recently been found in Egypt which mentions Knossos and Amnisos and perhaps Mycenàe. The list can be dated to the reign of Amenophis III (1417–1379).

Cretan products which have actually survived in the East are very few: some pots and stone vases. Farm produce probably supplemented this trade and perhaps tin and copper from Europe. We see as well from Egyptian tomb paintings that Minoans made gifts to the pharoahs of silver and gold Vafio cups and stone and metal bull's head rhyta (vases used for spreading liquids in rituals). In some of the tombs of high officials of the Egyptian court at Thebes in Upper Egypt these typically Minoan objects are shown being brought as presents to the pharoah by embassies of Syrians and of people called 'Keftiu'. Though it is not quite certain that all the Keftiu are Minoans, as the paintings form a series over the fifteenth and early fourteenth centuries, those in the earlier paintings definitely are: the profile with kisscurl and three thick strands of hair down the neck can be recognised in Knossos palace frescoes. In some of the later paintings Syrian-looking people, with hooked noses and ankle-length white linen gowns, are called Keftiu, or people who look like Minoans bring Syrian objects. We shall ignore the muddle which probably reflects the chauvinistic attitudes of the ancient Egyptians. Since in the early paintings there really are Minoans bringing Minoan objects, we can be confident that some embassies went from the court of Knossos to the court of Thebes. These embassies probably continued for as long as do the paintings purporting to show them, that is from the regency of Hatshepsut, mother of Thothmosis III (1504–1450) to the reign of Amenophis III (1417–1379), whom we have already found to be ruling at the time of the fall of Knossos (p. 19). That disaster doubtless ended the excursions.

Another equally important event in Cretan history, the change of control at Knossos in the mid-fifteenth century, may have been inadvertently recorded in a tomb painting. In the tomb of the Vizir Rekhmire, the Keftiu have been repainted. Originally they were shown with codpieces, part of the Minoan male dress, but these were altered to kilts, more appropriate to the Mycenaeans. One surmises that when one year the embassy that came from Knossos turned out not to be Minoans but Mycenaeans wearing different clothes, the artist was ordered to correct the picture.

We shall leave the history of the New Palaces for the moment to turn to their pottery, buildings and other achievements. Surprisingly, the earliest pottery, of Middle Minoan III, is disappointing and dull. Some of it followed the Kamares tradition in a stereotyped way, but much of it is a graceless dull brown. Evans explained the contrast with what had gone before by suggesting that the Minoans, or rather those in the palaces, were by now so rich that they were regularly using metalware on the table.

In the pottery of the succeeding phase, Late Minoan IA, there is a little more excitement, but still no sharp break in style. Vases are almost wholly in the dark-on-light mode, and decorated with spirals (Plate 6) and naturalistic plant designs. Spirals were particularly liked in East Crete where they remained in the repertoire when vases of the next phase, Late Minoan IB, were being imported from Knossos.

In Late Minoan IB the skills of the potters reached an excellence as high as that of Middle Minoan II. They could attempt virtually any shape of vase, and copied happily those of metal or stone. These shapes are sometimes extravagant, but usually they appear graceful and have a lively decoration. The plants of Late Minoan IA were painted more delicately in Late Minoan IB (Plate 7), and more refined formal patterns were introduced; but at the same time a rumbustious school of marine painting developed whose vases with googly-eyed octopuses swimming through seaweed and rocks and flanked by argonauts and nautili are some of the best known products of Minoan Crete. Among the marine and plant designs one can already recognise the work of individual painters. The principal home of the Late Minoan IB styles was Knossos, where the vase

7   This cup by the Olive Spray Painter shows Late Minoan IB painting at its most delicate. The hemispherical shape of the cup is one that was known since Old Palace times.

painters would have been stimulated by contact and competition with the fresco painters and the other palace craftsmen.

With Late Minoan II the mutual stimulus which the artists in the different techniques gave each other is still more obvious when bird scenes appeared on the pots: they had been part of the stock-in-trade of the fresco painters for some time already. The Late Minoan II style of pottery was confined to Knossos where, with the Mycenaeans in control, one or two shapes of vase were perhaps brought from the mainland. In decorating the vases there was a new approach which had already begun before the end of Late Minoan IB, of painting isolated motifs in an open field. This treatment is hardly known in the earlier history of Minoan pottery and may represent a change of spirit, but it is confined to the smaller vases. Large storage jars were still decorated in the traditional packed style, the octopuses being replaced by complex overall patterns of running spirals, palm trees and double axes. The styles of Late Minoan II developed into those of Late Minoan IIIA, a stiffer and more stylised version of what had gone before. Late Minoan IIIA is the style prevailing at the time that the Palace of Knossos was destroyed – to be precise, it happened when the Late Minoan IIIA1 style was changing to IIIA2, at about the end of the first quarter of the fourteenth century.

To what extent the buildings of the New Palaces had changed from those of the Old is difficult to tell, since so little is preserved of the Old Palaces. The best preserved Old Palace is at Phaistos: its architecture is considerably more sophisticated than one might have expected, which may mean that there was not much development in the New Palace period. Palaces at Ayia Triadha and

41

Zakro were apparently started from scratch; there had been no palaces before, although both places had long been inhabited.

Much survives of the towns of the time of the New Palaces: imposing town houses can be seen at Knossos, Phaistos, Ayia Triadha and Mallia and at Palaikastro, a burgherly town in East Crete where no palace has yet been found. Less grand towns of the time are Gournia, which is described below with Palaikastro, and Zakro and the off-shore islands of Mokhlos and Pseira.

The country houses are perhaps the most interesting development of the period, as they form an extension of the palace system to cover probably almost every area of the island. These country houses, or villas as they have often been called, are separated a few kilometres from each other and usually placed with a view over the plain or valley which the house controlled and from which it obtained its wealth. Even though the view was sometimes over the sea, all the Minoan country houses have an obvious geographical area around them which would have been their domain. Their architecture copies features of the palaces, such as ashlar masonry or pillar basements, or the use of gypsum. Some country houses should be thought of as ducal mansions, but others are no more than large farmhouses. Their owners imported fine vases from Knossos and oddities from abroad. They used stoneware and bronze implements indistinguishable from those used in the palaces, and had seals and clay tablets written in Linear A (Plate 8) to certify their claims to the produce which they stored in their ample storerooms, perhaps before remitting part of it to a palace. The rise of the country houses reflects the growth of a landed gentry (presumably much as happened in England or in the Veneto many centuries later), part of whose work was local administration.

Linear A inscriptions have been found at many places in Crete on clay tablets (Plate 8), and on stone and metal objects, and outside Crete, on Thera, Kea, Kythera and Melos, and as single signs on the Greek mainland. These inscriptions from outside Crete are very important evidence of how widespread Minoan influence was at the time.

Linear A seems to have replaced the Hieroglyphic script at about the time of the transition from the Old to the New Palaces. It gave way in turn to Linear B, an adaptation of the Minoan script to the Greek language at the probable conquest of Crete by the Greeks in the middle of the fifteenth century.

If Linear A, or the Hieroglyphic script, were to be deciphered, we could tell more of the origins of the Minoans. All that we know now is that there is a syllabic language (or languages) with ideograms, numerals and fractions like Linear B, and that the documents in it are mostly accounts or tax returns. Some inscriptions are cut on tables of offering and other objects connected with religion, and they should be prayers or imprecations. There is nothing to suggest that there is any literature in Linear A. As for deciphering it, the two most popular theories are that it is either a Semitic language or derived from Asia Minor. Neither can yet be proved.

Writing, fresco painting, and other decorative arts were all skills that emanated from the palaces in this period. Plenty of frescoes have survived from Knossos, Ayia Triadha and elsewhere in Crete – though surprisingly few from Phaistos; and outside Crete they have been found on Thera, Melos, Kea and

8 A broken Linear A tablet found in what may have been a shrine in the country
house at Pyrgos was probably an inventory or a tax return. It records 90 units (the
nine horizontal bars at the end of the second line) of wine (the sign before them)
which can be elucidated with the help of Linear B. The rest cannot be deciphered.

Rhodes. They are almost all executed in the true fresco technique, that is painted
on walls when the plaster was still wet; often one can see the marks of a string
impressed in the wet plaster to guide the painter. Although they are such an
important part of Minoan palatial life, the study of them has been neglected
until recently, so that any remarks here may be premature until new studies
have been published. However even now careful attention to the frescoes will
enrich one's understanding and enjoyment of the palaces. All the frescoes I shall
discuss are from Knossos, unless they are specifically said to be from somewhere
else.

Four styles predominate. First there are the frescoes with scenes in miniature
or on a reduced scale. The miniatures show packed crowds attending religious
ritual, bull games and dancing performances: the paintings are quick and lively;
features are shown by impressionist blobs, which in a simple range of colours
tell the essentials of the story. The pictures on a reduced scale include the so-
called Captain of the Blacks, a fresco reconstructed to show a white officer
leading some black soldiers at the double, and some recently found chariot
scenes which were probably painted in the Mycenaean phase at Knossos,
Late Minoan II and IIIAI. The second group of frescoes consists of formal
patterns on a larger scale, such as the rosettes (and later the spirals painted
over them) in the Queen's Room (p. 79), or the maeander patterns in the
niches at the North end of the Central Court at Phaistos. These frescoes show

the same attitudes as so much of the decoration of the pottery of the time.

The third and fourth groups are those with life size scenes of humans and animals. Humans are posed more formally than the animals, as one might expect, but any tendency to stiffness is usually corrected by the lively way in which people are drawn – a blend of manners with individual character that may reflect something of the mood of the Minoan court. You can see both these traits in the so-called Camp Stool fresco, of which the fresco of a woman known as La Parisienne forms part. As the Camp Stool fresco has been reconstructed, two rows of women of the court are shown sitting in pairs on stools, toasting each other or perhaps drinking to a divinity. They may be under the control of a priestess, who was christened La Parisienne by the workmen when they found her; but she may equally be a goddess to whom they are drinking. She is the central figure, being twice the size of the other women (despite the restoration in the Heraklion Museum) – as you can see yourself by extending the rest of her in your imagination from the part preserved, which is shown separately. Do not be surprised that she occupies two rows: this is a literal way of treating important people which was often used by Egyptian artists. What is unusual about her, however, is her coy smile and seductive look which transcend the formal structure of the painting. Another fresco which is similar to those of Egypt is the large Procession Fresco, a long parade of people carrying offerings which ran along the Corridor of the Procession starting from the West Porch. The people in the fresco carry gifts which are presumably for the king, priest or divinity of Knossos. When (real) people entered the palace along this corridor, they would have found the people in the picture accompanying them and likewise bringing gifts or tokens of respect. The tokens are typical products of the time of the New Palaces. This fresco belongs to the same *genre* as the Egyptian tomb paintings we have discussed earlier with Keftiu bearing gifts to the pharoah (p. 40). At both Knossos and Egyptian Thebes the men have bare bodies, with black hair dressed in three long curls and a kiss curl on the forehead, and wear a tartan codpiece or kilt. The racial type is the same, with a small forehead, hooked nose and a pinched-in waist.

The frescoes with animal and plant scenes are the most delightful of the Minoan pictures and may do most to show that Minoan Crete was a civilised place to live. There are sea-scenes: the best is the dolphin floor from a shrine at Ayia Triadha (p. 107). There are animals sporting in the flower strewn meadows of Crete in the springtime, a cat hunting, a monkey picking crocuses, birds such as the partridges from the Caravanserai (p. 86) and the doves from the House of the Frescoes (p. 85). People who could well be divine are occasionally included among the animals: a burnt fresco from Ayia Triadha shows a large woman sitting in a garden of flowers, who is probably a goddess of nature. Some animal scenes are dynamic rather than delightful, such as the charging bull from the North Portico (p. 59) which has been modelled in relief to give extra emphasis. It is an awesome animal. Like the quieter pictures, it shows the Minoans' keen awareness of the world around them.

The liveliness and the humour of this painting of nature – even the humour of the court scenes – were not confined to these frescoes, although they had more scope because of the larger scale. We have noticed the octopuses and sea creatures painted on Late Minoan IB pottery, the birds in Late Minoan II, and the plants and flowers that run through the pottery of the time of the New Palaces (Plate 7). The spirit is found similarly in the miniature art of the sealstones, and in metalware (compare the rampaging bull on one of the Vafio cups with the bull relief fresco from the North Portico). As for the court scenes and their religious overtones, there is a fascinating parallel to the frescoes in the painted decoration on the limestone sarcophagus from Ayia Triadha. Its panels show double axes on poles in stands – as they would have been outside the store-rooms at Knossos (Plate 15) – and an altar in front of a shrine which is decorated with a spiral fresco (like the spiral fresco in the Queen's Room of Knossos). The artist has included animals, which may in fact have been allowed to roam around the palaces as sacred beasts. A bull is being brought for sacrifice: two women, perhaps priestesses, perhaps princesses, or both, are coming in a chariot at one end, and two goddesses in another chariot at the other end, drawn by a griffin. On three sides doves hover in the air, and below the bull are two ibexes, or *agrimia*, the wild goats of Crete. The pictures have a serene and timeless atmosphere, sacred and strange but also natural and soothing.

The stonevase makers of the time of the New Palaces could also produce spirited works. Their masterpieces are a group of vases carved in relief. Some of these from Knossos have been preserved only as fragments carved with octopuses or as lions; but the most complete examples are three vases from Ayia Triadha and one from Zakro, which complement the pictures of Minoan life in the frescoes. The grandest of them is the Mountain Shrine Rhyton from Zakro, which was originally covered with gold leaf. It has a giddy scene of ibexes romping on a rocky mountain while some are climbing onto the shrine built on the summit. By contrast the Chieftain Cup from Ayia Triadha has a mock-heroic, mock-court scene with children playing at being young princes with an officer and three soldiers.

The two other relief vases from Ayia Triadha are less stiff. On the Harvester Vase a noisy crowd of peasants sing their way home from the olive harvest, holding the rods for beating the olives from the trees – as vivid and immediate as the crowds in the Miniature Frescoes. The Boxer Vase shows the energetic fighting and wrestling of the Minoan aristocracy at play.

Our account of the arts of the New Palaces will end with their faience and ivory, as some of the masterpieces of the Minoans are made of these materials. Ivory was used in many ways: graceful figurines such as the acrobat from Knossos, or something more dumpy, such as the naturalistic partridge pendant found in recent excavations near the Royal Road of Knossos. Boxes were made from ivory, and combs and pins. Of faience the most remarkable pieces are the Middle Minoan III treasures of the beginning of the New Palace period buried in the so-called Temple Repositories at Knossos (Plate 18). Among them are vases and sprays of flowers, but the finest works are the well-known figurines of goddesses who look and are dressed like La Parisienne: bare bosoms with a low-cut blouse, a flaring long skirt, long hair done in three tresses at the back tied with a large bow which may have had some holy connotation – Evans called this bow the 'sacral knot' – and a kiss curl on the forehead. In their hands they hold snakes and on the head of one of them doves are perched. They are shown in the Heraklion Museum as they were found, with sea shells scattered at their feet.

The riches buried in the Temple Repositories were probably offered originally at a palace shrine. They belong to the first half of the sixteenth century. Thereafter we have only a few indications, from scraps among the debris, of how rich Knossos was in its heyday, until around the time of its destruction many valuable goods were buried in the tombs of royalty and nobility. The finds at the other palaces however – and especially at Ayia Triadha and at the perhaps unlooted palace of Zakro – enable one to guess what the palace of Knossos must have contained. Luckily the architecture of Knossos is still preserved to us; and, as we shall see, the magnificence of it will correct any misconceptions one might have formed from the relative meagreness of the finds during the half century before the destructions of around 1450.

These destructions overwhelmed all the palaces and country houses in Crete except Knossos – though even here buildings outside the palace were destroyed – and possibly Khania. The Minoan centres burnt down – in fires so fierce that at Mallia mudbricks were baked and elsewhere pottery was vitrified – and were abandoned. The palace of Knossos seems to have survived to rule alone until it also was burnt down two or three generations later, in about 1375 when the Late Minoan IIIA1 style of pottery was changing to Late Minoan IIIA2. In the meantime some of the old centres had been re-inhabited and partly rebuilt – those of Phaistos, Ayia Triadha, Mallia, Tylissos, Gournia and Palaikastro – but the scale of life was smaller and this resettlement came only after a gap of some years. Clearly the effect of the 1450 destructions was shattering. The Minoan social order was smashed, and people died, or fled we do not know where, till the time of resettlement. One can understand at once the enhanced importance of a Knossos that survived, and was almost certainly under the rule of Greeks from the mainland.

The evidence for Greek rule consists of changes in the culture of the phases Late Minoan II – IIIA1/2 (1450–1375): new shapes in the potters' repertoire, such as the stemmed goblet, which may be of mainland origin; the greater use of *lapis lacedaimonius*, imported from near Sparta – blocks of it were waiting to be worked at Knossos (p. 80. **41**) when the palace was destroyed; a large number of tombs around Knossos, Phaistos and Ayia Triadha, something which would not be surprising if it were not that so few have been found from the period before – some of the tombs are vaulted tholos tombs, a style which could have come from the mainland, though it may originally be Minoan; and the appearance of a spirit of militarism for the first time in Crete, with chariot scenes and soldiers on frescoes, warriors – perhaps Mycenaean squires – buried with their sets of weapons as if in full dress uniform, and military equipment listed on the Linear B tablets. The language of the Linear B tablets of Knossos is the most important evidence of all of the probable change of power, since it has been deciphered to be, on the whole, Greek. When all this evidence is considered together, the most natural explanation is that Mycenaean Greeks were the masters of Knossos and, if so, the most likely time for them to have arrived was at or after the 1450 destructions.

We must still decide what caused the destructions. I think that they were probably the work of the Mycenaeans, who rampaged through Crete burning down its palaces and country houses but leaving the palace of Knossos, though some of the town houses there suffered. Earthquakes are also a possibility; and some people have suggested that the eruption of the volcano of Thera spewed volcanic ash over Crete. Thera, however, probably erupted some fifty years earlier (as only Late Minoan IA pottery has been found in that island's latest deposits) and there is no satisfactory evidence yet to connect it with the 1450 destructions.

Attacks from the mainland equally fit the evidence of the decline of Minoan influence in the Aegean at this time. Trianda on Rhodes was destroyed at the end of Late Minoan IB, and Phylakopi on Melos a little later at about the same time as Kastri on Kythera and Ayia Irini on Kea were abandoned (their exacavators suggest as a result of earthquakes). In Late Minoan II these two settlements were deserted, and so also may Phylakopi and Trianda have been. When resettlement came, the culture was more Mycenaean than Minoan. There had been a swing of power and a gradual Minoan withdrawal from the Aegean.

The Linear B tablets reveal how the Mycenaean rulers of Knossos, or their Minoan clerks, ran the island. That it was a bureaucracy had long been established by looking at the ideograms – simple pictures of the subject of the tablet, perhaps for the convenience of illiterate porters – but nobody was

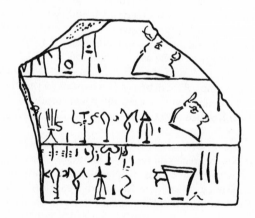

9 Part of a tablet from Knossos written in Linear B Greek. The strongest evidence that Myceaean Greeks were in control of Knossos when the palace was destroyed.
Linear B, the earliest form of Greek, is a syllabary and its signs have no connection with the alphabet of Classical Greek, which was of Phoenician origin. This tablet has part of a list of precious vases: decorated bull's-head rhyta, and silver cups with gold rims of the Vafio shape of Plate 6. The ideograms, or picture-signs, would have helped an illiterate porter to classify the documents.

expecting before the decipherment quite how meticulous it would prove to be. The tablets record payments, including deficits and surpluses, and inventories in farm produce and livestock, textiles, spices, metalwork, pottery, horses, chariots, military equipment, and even in offerings to the gods (to be stored in their treasuries) (Plate 9). Chariots, for instance, are broken up into their components, like the spare parts in a modern car catalogue; and places all over Crete are mentioned as having to pay to Knossos. The control is minute, and would have needed plenty of local commissioners. As it is so sophisticated, it is a reasonable assumption that it was not a wholly new system introduced by the Mycenaeans, but rather that the existing Minoan system and Minoan civil service had been adapted for the new Greek language and the people who spoke it.

The society that the tablets reveal is very much what we might have expected from considering the archaeological evidence: there is a king (*wanax*) with lords beneath him, all of whom have their own estates, and a large number of different types of craftsmen and agricultural workers who were probably independent artisans and peasants, and slaves. Little is said about the organisation of the Knossian army, despite the details of its kit, though there was a man called the 'leader of the people' or 'leader of the host' who may have been head of the army.

The language of the tablets is a primitive Greek, but it would be very useful to find a large archive of new texts to confirm the decipherment as Greek. Some words in Linear B cannot easily be fitted into our knowledge of classical Greek and others are of Hittite or Semitic origin. The word for ivory is derived from Hittite (the precursor of our word 'elephant'), and those for gold, linen and some spices come from a Semitic language. These foreign words probably confirm that there was trade in these commodities, but they could have been adopted into the language of Crete at a much earlier date.

The information in the Linear B tablets, the quality of goods buried in the tombs and the finds in the palace debris of Knossos reveal that life continued to be prosperous, and foreign luxuries were still being imported. Embassies may still have gone from Knossos to the court of the pharoahs, though staffed now by Mycenaeans (p. 40).

About 1375 B.C. Knossos burnt to the ground, the flames fanned by a South wind: you can still see the marks on the West facade and elsewhere in the palace (Plate 15). We do not know why it happened. It may have been a rebellion by the native Minoans against their Mycenaean overlords. Or perhaps the Mycenaeans of Knossos were revolting against those on the mainland, and this led to a cutting-out expedition to destroy for ever a still powerful Knossos. Or there may have been another earthquake. We cannot tell. In some of those grand tombs may be buried the kings and nobles who were caught in the troubles, but were still given the last rites and buried with the possessions around them which they had enjoyed in life.

The palaces of Knossos became a ruin, and in time people camped in its ghostly remains. Something of the zest for life was gone in Crete, and the island became a backwater, removed from the mainstream of Aegean culture for several hundreds of years.

4 Visiting the Palaces

The accounts that follow of the palaces and the town and country houses of Crete are intended primarily to give guidance to visitors as they go around the buildings. I hope they will also help both readers and visitors to understand more of the Minoan life and work in these magnificent buildings – which I have been trying to explain in the previous chapters – and to see how archaeologists unravel their secrets, and even to reconstitute what Minoan buildings were like before they were destroyed.

Some practical points:

1   The rooms of the palaces and houses are numbered on the different systems of the different excavations. Knossos has never been numbered. I have followed these different systems, and for Knossos I have numbered myself the key points in the tour. Numbers are shown in the text in bold type: e.g. the Room of the Stirrup Jars at Knossos **15**, or the Peristyle Hall at Phaistos **74**.

I have kept most of Evans's names for the rooms of Knossos, which can be found also on notices in the palace. These notices are in English, French and Greek and often say something different in each language. The English text is to be preferred, as it is usually what Evans christened the room.

I have called storerooms 'storerooms' and not 'magazines' and raised walks 'raised walks' and not 'causeways'. I have used 'pillar crypt' when I think a basement with pillars standing in it to support the room above may itself have had some religious use (such as at Knossos, p. 71, Fig. 6.**25**): otherwise I have called these rooms 'pillar basements'.

2   Knossos, Phaistos, Mallia and Gournia are aligned North to South; Zakro is a little off the meridian. Be sure which end is which – easy enough in the Cretan sun – as the descriptions and tours are based on the points of the compass.

3   The houses, and almost everything visible in the palaces, belong to the time of the New Palaces. The few remains that are Prepalatial or of the Old Palace period will be identified as such.

4   Phaistos, Ayia Triadha, Mallia, Amnisos, Nirou Khani, Tylissos, Mitropolis, Arkhanes, Vathypetro can all be visited easily from Heraklion, but spend a night if you can at the simple Tourist Pavilion at Phaistos. It is unforgettable there at sunset and in the early morning. For the sites in East Crete stay at Ayios Nikolaos or Sitia, a pleasant town which deserves to be visited more. All the sites mentioned are fairly easily accessible, but the last part of the road to Ano Zakro and Zakro may be still very bad. However, I have found that all roads in Crete are negotiable if you go slowly enough.

Most visitors start at Knossos, as it is so close to Heraklion. By going there first, you will have a clearer idea from the reconstructions how the other palaces would have looked; but I urge you to return to Knossos after you have visited the others. You will then appreciate the grandeur of Knossos and see that it was indisputably the capital of Minoan Crete.

5 Knossos

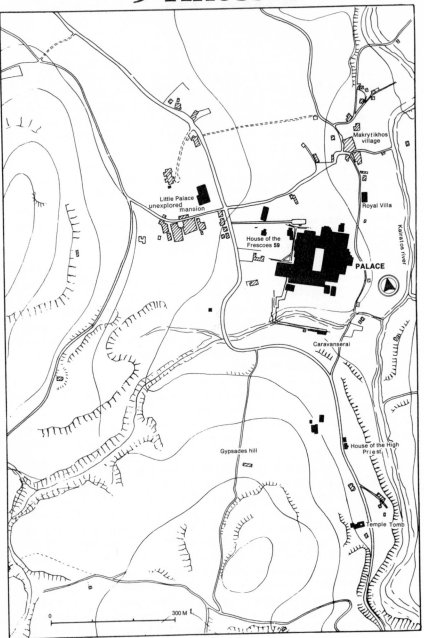

Fig. 5. The area round the Palace of Knossos.

The palace at Knossos is not on the sea as is Heraklion, the modern business capital of Crete, nor is it on a commanding hill as is Phaistos; and it is not easy to imagine that the Kairatos stream below the palace (Fig. 5) was ever broad enough to carry boats. Visitors are often surprised that this comparatively low and inland position on a shelf jutting out from the West side of the valley should have been chosen as the site of what became the capital of Minoan Crete. When however the first Neolithic settlers noticed the spot in the seventh millennium, it was then a hill set *in* the valley at the highest point where there is such a hill. The flat site you see today is the result of levelling the western slope of this hill in Middle Minoan II times to create the wide West Court across which you now approach the palace. The advantages the Neolithic people saw in the hill were that it was near the sea, but far enough away to give time to escape from pirates or invaders; it had convenient supplies of fresh water from the Kairatos (and, later, from wells) and there was rich farming land around; it was also near higher ground in case they did need a refuge; and finally the position of Knossos with regard to the rest of the island was as central then as that of Heraklion is today. You will see this if you climb the hills around the palace: much of Crete is spread before you, from Psiloriti to the Lasithi mountains, with the sea to the North, and to the South the passes that lead over to the plain of Mesara.

The palace of Knossos is large and complicated (Fig. 6). You appreciate how large it is when you return to Knossos after looking at the other palaces: it is twice the size of Phaistos and Mallia, four times that of Zakro and seven times that of the small palace at Gournia. Knossos more than any other of the palaces seems a glorified village in which many different activities were carried on in separate and hidden parts of the building. Unlike the New Palaces at Phaistos and Mallia, it does not look as if it was planned as a whole at any one time. For this reason, and because of the difficulty of digging a place with so many layers superimposed, the architectural history of Knossos is a huge problem; but with many details preserved, it will repay the effort to try to see what did happen. If you make the effort, your visits to Knossos will be more interesting and more enjoyable.

Many of the details which make Knossos so fascinating have been preserved and developed by Evans in his work of restoration or, as he called it, 'reconstitution'. These restorations have often been criticised, as people have thought them ugly – but they are of enormous help in understanding Knossos, which would otherwise be an incomprehensible mess: and by understanding Knossos, you can understand better the other palaces which have not been restored. For Evans his 'reconstitutions' were essential to complete the work, as he had to shore up what had already been uncovered before proceeding down. The rotted timbers in the timber-and-rubble walls had dissolved the walls into heaps of stones and made excavation unsafe and the stratigraphy complicated. Evans has normally preserved the evidence for his reconstitutions: I hope readers will find, as I have found, that the closer you look, the more you marvel at how accurate and honest he was. Equally, his landscaping of the ruins shows style and imagination, as you will see if you walk on the hills around Knossos. What might seem from inside the palace the random placing of the restored parts appears from afar a pleasing and harmonious whole.

10   The West Court **1** of Knossos was levelled and laid in Middle Minoan II. It is crossed by raised walks, one of which runs from the Theatral Area **6** along the West facade past an altar base to the West Entrance and Porch **3** from where this photograph was taken. The line of larger stones between the walk and the altar base probably marks where the facade of the Old Palace had been, farther out than the present New Palace facade, as at Phaistos (Plate 24). When you look at the gypsum blocks of the facade, you will see the fire marks of the destruction of the palace in about 1375. They show that the wind was blowing from the South.

Entering the Palace

The visitor approaches the palace of Knossos (Fig. 6) through a modern entrance and along a meandering trellissed path that crosses the dip which originally lay between the palace hill and the West side of the valley to arrive finally at the West Court **1**. You can see the Minoan ramp across this dip in the cutting beside the path. As you reach the modern concrete bridge, stop, and look at the large paved area of the West Court, with its retaining wall immediately in front of you. It dates from Middle Minoan II (1800–1625) when the Court was levelled up, and at the far side of the Court is the monumental West facade of the later New Palace. You will notice at once that the crazy paving of the Court is crossed by raised walks which direct the visitor like a red carpet either straight ahead to the West Entrance **3**, or left to the North-West corner of the palace and the so-called Theatral Area **6** further along the West facade (Plate 10). These raised walks are typical of Minoan architecture: at Mallia and at Phaistos you will see similar formal paths raised above the paved Western approaches, insisting on ways of entrance and exit. One has recently been found crossing the Court at the country house at Pyrgos on the South coast (Plate 46).

Another distinctive feature of the West Courts of Knossos, Phaistos and

11   Part of the Central Court and West wing of Knossos, soon after discovery. Much of what you see here was later roofed by Evans.

Mallia are large circular pits (often called *koulouras*, a Greek word referring to things round and hollow). At Knossos there are three *koulouras* **2** inside the railings to your left, as you enter the Court. You can see at the bottom of them house remains of the last phase before the foundation of the Old Palace, Middle Minoan IA (2050–1900). The interior fittings of these prepalatial houses are made of red plaster. Later, when the West Court was levelled during the later part of the life of the Old Palace, these pits were built up and the houses left at the bottom. The pits may have been intended to be granaries – the ones at Mallia (Plate 32) almost certainly are – or perhaps they were for sacred offerings. In time at any rate they were filled with potsherds and rubbish.

Follow the raised walk straight ahead which leads behind the bust of Evans towards the West Entrance **3**. (To the South, that is to your right, are some remains of mainly Late Minoan III houses, belonging to the time after the palace had been destroyed in about 1375.) About 2 m. in front of the West facade you notice a line of larger slabs in the paving (Plate 10) which are probably part of the facade of the Old Palace: it is likely that the facade was moved back from this line when the New Palace was built, to make room for the West Entrance and its porch. At Phaistos there is a much better example of taking the facade back (Plate 24). Opposite where you now stand stretches the beautifully finished monumental West facade of the New Palace, on which you can still see the fire marks which show that the wind was blowing from the South when the palace burnt down. Between the Old Palace slabs in the pavement and the New Palace facade is an altar base, which would mark the holiness of the entrance to the palace. Behind the altar base you will notice an indent in the facade which is probably evidence that there was a window on the upper storey set in the recess.

This detail, the line of the wall slightly inset, often recurs in Minoan architecture: when measured, these recesses are usually found to be in the middle of the supposed rooms on upper floors. The most likely explanation of them is that they held the windows in what would be the appropriate place for them, between the partitions.

The West wall of the palace of Knossos is now in front of you. It is faced outside and inside with gypsum blocks, now turned white by time and the elements, but originally grey, crystalline and shiny. They had probably been quarried on the hill of Gypsades ('Gypsum Hill') which rises immediately on the other side of the small valley to the South of the Palace. These blocks were held together by crossbeams of wood (you can see the dovetail mortice-holes from inside some of the Storerooms) and filled with a core of stone rubble. The resulting wall was strong and yet elastic, well suited for an earthquake zone. The inside surfaces of the gypsum blocks were left rough but, even so, some of them were engraved with double axes and other signs, marking the sanctity of the place. You can see signs on the inside faces of the blocks enclosing the wall between Storerooms 2 and 5. Before you go into the West Entrance, notice that the wall rests on a slightly projecting bottom course, the levelling course. It is a common feature in Minoan buildings, but usually is not as wide as here.

The West Entrance and Porch 3 reveal at once many of the intricacies of Minoan buildings. A raised walk approaches the Entrance diagonally from the North, meets the raised walk from the West, by which we have come, and leads us inside, twisting slightly to the right around the main supporting column of the Porch and then to the left through a door into the Porch, which is a room with a red plaster floor. Already we have experienced the lack of a direct way through, a favourite conceit of Minoan architects. Instead, there is a dogleg approach which is at once more bewildering. Here in this first room there may have been a preliminary check, and beside it may be a guardroom. Go now through the double doors at the East end of the Porch (they are marked by sockets where the two door posts stood and a small peg hole in the middle where the doors were fastened) and along the Corridor of the Procession Fresco 4. This Corridor has fallen away at the South, but there is now a false way to the East (your left) from just before where it falls away, over walls, to reach the Propylaea 21. We shall ignore this false entrance.

The Corridor of the Procession Fresco was originally a long and oblique approach to the main part of the palace: it turned East at the South-West corner of the palace and ran above basements which are still visible on the South side of the palace. Off this (now vanished) South part of the Corridor of the Procession Fresco one could turn back to the North to come into the Propylaea 21, ascend Staircase 20 and so reach the main rooms of the West side. If one did not turn off here, one could continue a few more metres and again turn left, following the Corridor, and come out at the Central Court. This is where the so-called Priest King Fresco has been restored. When you come later to that part of the palace (p. 83), you will notice that the paving is still the same as in the West part of the Corridor: gypsum flagstones with blue schist crazy paving set in red plaster – a typically Minoan contrast of colours and textures. The figure known as the Priest King may in fact be a woman and a priestess, to judge from the white colour of the body and the feminine hairstyle: she would have been leading the long Procession of the Fresco, which then ran the length of the Corridor from the West Entrance 3. Little of the Fresco is left, but enough shows that a long procession was bringing presents to the god or the king (or both, since it is not easy to distinguish between human and divine or sacred and secular in Minoan palaces). This type of scene is known in contemporary Egypt and was copied from Crete by the Mycenaeans, who adopted much of the Minoan icono-graphy for their frescoes when they began to build palaces, probably in the fourteenth century. These scenes show the ceremonial life of the court, and it is most interesting to compare their pictures of objects with actual examples of them.

The effect on the visitor to the palace of such frescoes should have been that of awe. As he walked into the building, he was among the figures of the procession and became one of them. He could well have been bringing gifts, as they were; and they led him either to the Central Court, where a priestess probably headed the procession, or to grand reception rooms on the first floor of the West side of the palace. Among these rooms was a treasury for sacred offerings.

We must leave the Corridor of the Procession Fresco since it can no longer take us into the palace. Instead we shall return the way we came back through the West Entrance 3 and out into the West Court 1 and follow the raised walk running North along the West facade. At the North end of the Court is another altar base. If you turn here and look back along the West facade, you have a striking view of how thick a wall it is. Continuing North you come down to the Theatral Area 6 just beyond the North-West corner of the palace, where there may have been another Entrance 5.

The Theatral Area 6 was probably used to receive important visitors or, as has been recently suggested, to try cases at law. It has a paved courtyard at the foot of shallow steps or terraces which would have held a crowd of standing spectators (the West Court of the Old Palace at Phaistos (Plate 26) has similar steps). If you stand in the middle, on the South side (to your left) is a raised rectangle which could have been the base of a wooden royal box, or something similar, while in front of you stretches the Royal Road 7. The actual road is in fact another raised walk which leads to the Little Palace (p. 87) 250 m. away. As excavated, it is in a defile, but originally it was lined with buildings, which seem to have been quite elegant houses built over workshops and studios on their ground floors. If you approach the Theatral Area along the Royal Road, you will find that another raised walk branches off to the right running behind the possible Royal Box and past the remains of a gypsum horns of consecration (a sacred symbol of stylised bull's horns which was often placed along the eaves of Minoan buildings) to the North Entrance 8 of the palace (and yet another runs off this one probably to the North Pillar Crypt 9, a shrine built outside the North Entrance).

Before you leave the Theatral Area, climb up to its top terrace and look over the back. There you can see evidence of an earlier, and different, arrangement before the present terraces were built: beneath them is a paved courtyard with an earlier raised walk leading to the North Entrance, and another pavement which may be earlier still as it is on a lower level. In this earlier courtyard was a

Fig. 6. Plan of the Palace of Knossos.

1 West Court
2 *Koulouras*
3 West Entrance and Porch
4 Corridor of the Procession Fresco
5 North-West Entrance (?)
6 Theatral Area
7 Royal Road
8 North Entrance
9 North Pillar Crypt
10 North-West Hall and Portico
11 Bath in **10**
12 North Pillar Hall
13 Keep
14 Room of the Staffron Gatherer Fresco
15 Room of the Stirrup Jars
16 Corridor of the Stone Basin
17 Throne Room suite
18 Staircase up from the Central Court
19 Propylon
20 Staircase
21 Propylaea
22 Lobby of the Stone Seat
23 Room of the Tall Pithos
24 Temple Repositories
25 Pillar Crypts
26 Vat Room
27 Long Corridor of the Storerooms
28 Grand Staircase
29 Corridor of the Bays
30 Storeroom of the Medallion Pithoi
31 Corridor of the Draughtboard
32 Hall of the Colonnades
33 Corridor to the East (East-West Corridor)
34 Hall of the Double Axes
35 Queen's Room
36 Corridor of the Painted Pithos
37 Dressing Room
38 Court of the Distaffs
39 Service staircase
40 East Portico
41 Storeroom below stone vase maker's workshop
42 'School Room'
43 Court of the Stone Spout
44 Storeroom of the Giant Pithoi
45 North-East Hall
46 North-East Storerooms
47 Pens for animals (?)
48 East Bastion
49 Corridor of the Sword Tablets
50 Shrine of the Double Axes
51 Passage of the Lily Jars
52 South Entrance
53 House of the Sacrificed Oxen
54 House of the Fallen Blocks
55 House of the Chancel Screen
56 South-East House
57 House of the Monolithic Pillars
58 South House
59 House of the Frescoes

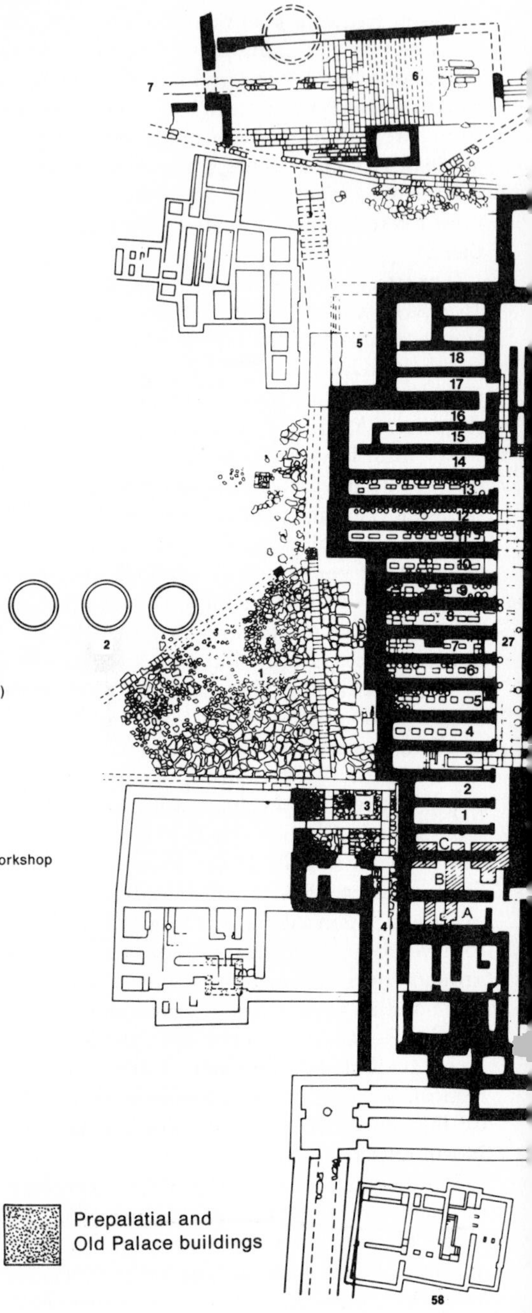

NB **53**, **54**, **59** and **9** are not shown.
but **59** is in Fig. 5.

Prepalatial and
Old Palace buildings

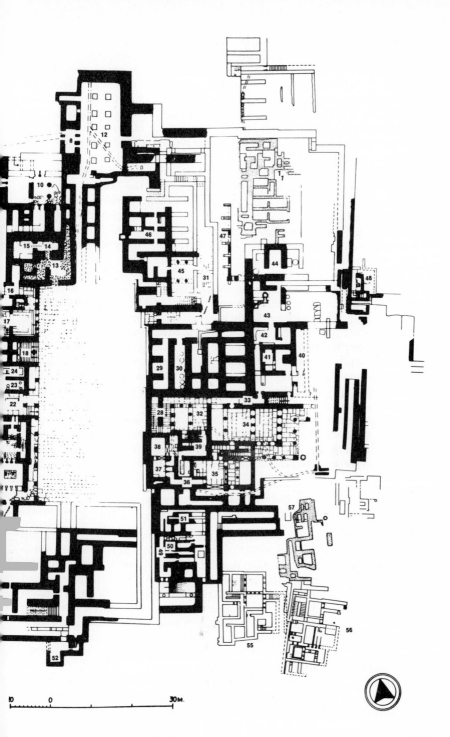

10   0   30м.

57

kouloura pit, like those in the West Court. It cannot be seen now, but it lies in the confines of the present Theatral Area, below the low wall on its North side.

Leaving the Theatral Area, go to the North Entrance **8**, where the tour inside the palace will really begin. You first pass a projecting part: little is preserved, but there is a gypsum facade with a rubble filling behind built in the same way as the West facade. In the middle is a side entrance into a passage or verandah, and through double doors you go into the North-West Hall and its Portico **10**. (These double doors are shown by the same type of door sockets as we saw in the West Entrance. You will soon be familiar with these sockets which show where the doors were set, and with the jambs which show how they opened, always inwards from the cross-piece of the jamb.) The Hall is of a typical Minoan style, divided into areas by piers, which were commonly used for internal room division instead of columns. The doors set against the piers, or rather against the jambs of the piers, opened inwards and folded back like shutters. The Minoans used such arrangements often to make one large room or two small ones, and to adjust the light, warmth and ventilation.

Through these double doors you come at the North-West corner of the Hall to a Bath **11**, now restored and so seeming to stand free. The Bath is sunken and has steps down into it. At Knossos there are other baths like this inside the palace and in the grand houses around, and they can also be seen at Phaistos, Mallia, Zakro and Tylissos. Evans called them 'Lustral Basins', thinking that they were used primarily for ritual purification: he pointed out that they could not have been filled with water since there is no outlet for the dirty water. However, one could have put a clay bath in them, had it filled with water brought by slaves and hung curtains round the sides for privacy. Since the prime purpose of these rooms was cleansing, I shall call them Baths rather than Lustral Basins. All the same I agree with Evans and those who think that in buildings as redolent of divine rights as the Minoan palaces there was little distinction between physical and spiritual cleansing: to do the one would have been almost certainly the same as doing the other. This attitude can be illustrated from the Psalms:

> Thou shalt purge me with hyssop, and I shall be clean:
> thou shalt wash me, and I shall be whiter than snow.
>
> (Ps. 51. 7)

The Bath **11** in the North-West Hall (**10**) is larger and deeper than most, and its steps go round three sides, which is also unusual: steps on two sides are more common. It is well built, of ashlar, that is dressed limestone masonry, and has a gypsum dado, or facade, lining the walls and a gypsum floor. In the area beyond it Evans found the lid of a stone vase with the cartouche of the Egyptian pharaoh Khyan who reigned in the later seventeenth century. With the lid was pottery belonging to Middle Minoan IIIA, the earliest phase of the period of the New Palaces, which is a typical synchronism of the sort used to date the Minoan era. It also enables us to guess when this part of the palace was built, soon after the earthquakes that overthrew the Old Palace.

It is puzzling why this wing with its Bath and Hall was built here on the North edge of the palace, since it has only limited communication with the blocks to the South along a dogleg passage leading in dark, circuitous fashion to the Corridor of the Stone Basin **16** to the North of the Throne Room. (It is worth the walk up this passage to look over at the walls of the Keep **13** which will be described below, but do not fall in!) Evans suggested that the function of this wing was that people were purified here before entering the palace. He may well be right. One may imagine that it was a considerable ritual for a person to be made worthy to enter the palace precincts.

The North Entrance **8** is a small lobby with double doors either side, each opening inwards. Through it you enter the North Pillar Hall **12**, an imposing structure whose sturdy pillars were designed to support a large hall above. You will notice signs are carved on the blocks of the pillars, such as double axes or stars. They were either mason's marks or were used to sanctify the area, or were for both purposes, as the crosses on the stonework of medieval cathedrals are. These marks are quite common in the Minoan palaces. (About 20 m. outside to the North is a separate building, the North Pillar Crypt **9**. Like the larger North Pillar Hall **12**, the Crypt **9** served as the undercroft of a more important hall on the floor above. Evans thought that it may have been a shrine which people visited before they could reach the palace.)

South from the North Pillar Hall a ramp, the North Entrance Passage, leads up to the Central Court. Originally the ramp was wider than it is now but, during the life of the New Palace, it was narrowed when bastions were inserted, perhaps to support another large room above. A narrower ramp would also have been easier to guard. The ramp is built over the Keep **13**, of which you can see a wall through a grille in the ramp. The bastions on the East side of the ramp – to your left as you go up – have been left as they were found, but on the West they were restored as was the porch above them with the relief fresco of a charging bull which was found lying in pieces in the Entrance Passage below. Notice on the blocks below the porch more carved signs, here tridents and double axes. At the bottom of the ramp on the East side are gypsum door jambs and two peg holes which Evans took to mark the entrance of a porter's room, but they may as easily show the well of a wooden staircase to the presumed halls above. The ramp itself was open to the skies and, when it rained, water would have poured down it, spilling into a large drain which goes into the North Pillar Hall. There it meets another drain, which probably took the rainwater from the roof of the buildings in the North-East quarter of the palace, now one of the most ruined parts of the building.

The Keep **13** (marked by dots in the plan, Fig. 6), is a rectangular complex of monumentally high (or deep, as you see them now) walls forming small rooms which Evans thought originally to be dungeons. They may instead have been used as granaries, and in all events they made a piling against the North side of the hill of the Central Court to prevent the Old Palace's slipping down the hill. The Keep would have been dug into the layers of the Neolithic settlements. You may have already looked down at the Keep from the passage leading from the North-West Hall **10** to the Corridor of the Stone Basin **16**, but you can now see it to still better advantage from the wall at the North end of the Central Court, where iron grilles have been placed to prevent your falling in.

The New Palace rooms built over the Keep are of little architectural interest. They include a small shrine, the Room of the Saffron Gatherer Fresco **14** (this fresco was originally thought to show a boy collecting saffron, but he has now been identified as a monkey) and the Room of the Stirrup Jars **15**. In both these rooms Linear B tablets were found. The Room of the Stirrup Jars has been one of those at the heart of the recent controversy about the date of the final destruction of the palace: the specific argument has been whether the stirrup jars (closed jars, with a spout on the shoulder and stirrup-shaped handle on the top) in the Room, of Late Minoan IIIB (thirteenth century) type, were lying together with the tablets, in which case the vases would date them to Late Minoan IIIB, or whether the tablets were on a lower floor, and therefore earlier, as Evans thought. Both these rooms above the Keep were part of an area in the palace which included the rest of the North-East block which had been used for administration and records since the time of the Old Palace. Our evidence for this is the mass of records which have been found here: texts in Greek Linear B and Minoan Linear A scripts of the New Palace time and in the Hieroglyphic script belonging to the Old Palace. The Hieroglyphic texts were found in a cache under the stairs at the North end of the Long Corridor of the Storerooms **27**. It is clear that the idea began early of using this part of the palace for bureaucracy, adjacent to where the agricultural wealth was stored.

Besides what you see on the ground level, you can reconstruct something of the upper floor in this quarter. The thickened walls on the South and East sides of the dogleg passage from the North Portico to the Corridor of the Stone Basin indicate the outline of a room above. This room would have extended to the North Entrance Passage, the ramp which has a thickened wall on its West side, and could have been reached by stairs to the East of the dogleg passage. Finally, do not be puzzled that several rooms on the ground floor have no apparent entrances: they are basements which would have been reached through trap doors.

The Corridor of the Stone Basin **16** brings you from the Central Court to the North end of the Long Corridor of the Storerooms **27**. It is quite wide at first but narrows beyond the Keep. The purple stone basin, now in the Anteroom of the Throne Room (Plate 13), was found in it; but whether it was kept there during the life of the palace before its destruction and before parts of the ruins were reinhabited in the late thirteenth century is not known.

The Central Court

The Central Court measures about 50 × 25 m., which is equivalent to about 165 × 82½ Minoan feet, according to the calculations of J. W. Graham. (The Minoan foot he has found from measurements principally at Phaistos, Mallia and Zakro to be approximately 0.3036 m. or about one sixteenth of an inch shorter than the English foot.) The Central Court of Knossos is much the same size as those of Phaistos and Mallia. As it appears now it is mostly of plain earth, covered with flowers in the spring; but originally it was paved. Some of the paving is preserved in the North-West corner but, to imagine how it looked originally, you must see the Central Court at Phaistos. Like the paving, the walls around the Knossos Court have been mostly destroyed, but it seems that there were few openings along the North and South sides, while only on the

12　The Throne Room **17** of Knossos: the throne may not have been the seat of
Minos, but rather have been used by a priestess of the Minoan goddess. Its design
copies another throne of wood and seems to incorporate a sun-and-moon motif.
Griffins flank the throne and opposite it is a Bath, all evidence of the sanctity of the
Throne Room. From the scattered and overturned vases he found, Evans thought that
a ritual may have been happening when the great disaster came to Knossos.

West are there many surviving (Plate 11). These blank walls would have made
the Central Court seem more enclosed than the Courts of Phaistos and Mallia,
where starkness is relieved by porticos or cloisters.

The Throne Room suite **17** is by the North-West corner of the Central
Court. The Throne Room itself (Plate 12) is unique in the Minoan palaces –
several of the others have important rooms with benches which could have
been used for councils, but none has a room like this with benches around a
throne and with so many ancillary rooms. Evans thought the suite was inserted
into the palace in Late Minoan II, which could explain why the walls to the
North and West of the suite have been truncated – see Fig. 6 – and why the area
behind the Throne Room in the suite has no separate access. *If* this suite was built
in Late Minoan II, it is not surprising that there is nothing like it in the other
palaces, since they had all been destroyed at the end of Late Minoan IB: Late
Minoan II begins the period of mainland control at Knossos when the other
palaces were in ruins. All the same, even if there is nothing exactly like it
elsewhere and if it was built under Mycenaean Greek directions, the treatment
of the room is essentially in the native Minoan tradition: the benches, the
patterns of the floor, and even the fresco (restored though it is) are all what
one would expect in a Minoan palace built earlier in the New Palace period. As
for the lack of a separate access, this may be explicable if the Throne Room was
not in fact a room for the ceremonial seat of the king, but a shrine for which
separate access is inappropriate.

13   The Anteroom of the Throne Room. The stone basin was found outside in Corridor **16** to the North, but was early moved in here. The floor is similar to that in the Throne Room, crazy paving set in plaster surrounded by gypsum flagstones. The steps down into the Anteroom remind you that the Central Court is the top of what was originally a separate hill set in the valley.

From the Central Court step down into the Anteroom of the Throne Room (Plate 13): the steps remind you that the Central Court is the original top of what was a separate hill in the valley, which became a Neolithic and then a Minoan tell (like the tells, or city mounds, of the Near East). The Anteroom, like the Throne Room proper, has typical Minoan features: benches round the walls, and a floor of gypsum slabs surrounding a limestone crazy pavement with red plaster in the interstices. On the North side a mass of carbonised wood was found and here a wooden throne, on the model of that in the Throne Room, has been restored. As I have said, the stone basin in the centre was found in the Corridor of the Stone Basin **16** outside to the North.

The Throne Room (Plate 12) is an exciting spot, dark and mysterious but now alas fenced off because of damage from visitors. Its polished gypsum flagstones reflect the light that comes in from the bright Court, and the throne set against the wall has an odd, sinuous shape and decoration. Its design almost certainly copies an older throne of wood. Evans came upon the throne in the first days of his excavations in 1900 when the throne was found a few centimetres below the surface. Lying scattered on the floor of the Throne Room were large flat oil vases of gypsum and a storage jar (or *pithos*), which gave Evans the idea that some ritual was actually in progress when the palace was overwhelmed, perhaps to avert the impending disaster. The Bath the other side of the Room from the throne, which is also at the bottom of a light well, could have had a more specifically religious use here than, say, the one we have already seen at the North-West Hall **11**. His belief that ritual took place here is important as nothing has been found in the Throne Room to suggest that it was actually a room for kings, whereas the Hall of the Double Axes **34** (Plate 22) on the East side of the palace is much more suited for kingly purposes. It may rather be the case that this whole suite of the 'Throne Room' was a shrine where a priestess sat on the throne, perhaps as an epiphany of the goddess, attended by the divine griffins painted on the walls (the originals are in the Heraklion Museum). We have already noticed griffins on the painted sarcophagus from Ayia Triadha, where they are pulling a chariot with what are probably two goddesses inside.

At the back of the Throne Room are other rooms of the suite which are also shut off. They include two small service rooms to the West: in one is a fitted plaster table or platform which may have been used for preparing food or it may have been a table of offerings. In front of it a stone lamp stands on the floor. On the South side behind the Bath, cists (or lined strong-boxes set in the floor) are concealed under the main staircase **18** up from the Central Court.

We can leave the Anteroom of the Throne Room to go upstairs either by this staircase or we can take the small one at the North-East corner of the Throne Room suite. This corner you will see is rounded on the outside, which led Evans to date its construction to the Old Palace period. He thought it may have been an isolated block and the nearby Keep, which also has rounded corners, another; and that the palace may have begun as a collection of such blocks. The staircase inside this rounded corner leads to the reconstructed rooms above, and to an exhibition of copies of frescoes.

When you have walked through this small exhibition, you will come to what

14 The thicker wall between Storerooms 16 and 17 was clearly intended to be loadbearing and would have supported a wall dividing the rooms on the upper floor. Thicker walls and buttresses (Plates 15 and 19) are some of the clues to how the upper floor was planned.

would have been the rooms built over the long line of the Storerooms (which we have not yet visited). Here you can yourself reconstruct what these upper rooms would have been like by spotting where there are buttresses or where some of the walls on the ground floor are extra thick. These buttresses and thicker walls were designed to be loadbearing: so that from them one can produce a plan of the lost upper storey. Evans called this upper storey the *piano nobile*, as it was apparent to him from studying this evidence and from what he found fallen down into the rooms below that this level would have had the main reception rooms of the palace as the *piano nobile* does in an Italian Renaissance palace. Stand now at the North edge of the restoration (top right of the concrete platform) where you are on top of the wall between Storerooms 12 and 13, and you are in the middle of a large hall which would have occupied the whole projection on the West side of the palace from above Storeroom 11 to Storeroom 16, which are both defined by thicker walls. The small recess in the palace facade which we looked at earlier from the West Court can now be seen to be in the centre of this hall we have restored, above Storerooms 13 and 14 in the ground plan: it almost certainly marks the place of a window which has now unfortunately been put together in concrete in the wrong place (above Storerooms 11 and 12). But the column bases, which have been put in concrete where there are thinner walls below, are probably correctly placed where these internal supports actually were.

We can use the same principle of looking for thicker walls and other supports to reconstruct the other rooms that were over the Storerooms. There would have been a rather square room at the North-West corner over Storerooms 17 and 18 and the rest of the North-West corner of the palace.

Another room would obviously have been above Storerooms 10 to 6, and another above 5 to 3: both probably had central windows in recesses. You will notice also buttresses in Storerooms 7 and 9. They would have supported large columns in the room above, that over Storerooms 10 to 6; and, as one can see from the plan, they frame the window which we have restored in the central recess.

From the reconstructed upper storey you also have a good view down onto the West wall of the palace. The thick West wall is built, as we described earlier but which you can now see clearly, of gypsum slabs encasing a rubble core, the two faces bound together by wooden beams. This method of construction gave strength and elasticity, in case of earthquake.

The Storeroom walls are made by the more usual rubble-and-timber method, that is rubble packed between timbers (still used in Turkish times in Crete), but are faced with gypsum orthostats (vertical slabs) where they front onto the Long Corridor of the Storerooms 27. Many slabs are engraved with double axe signs, and small stone pyramids which held double axes on poles were found outside the different Storerooms (Plate 15): standards like these are shown on the painted sarcophagus from Ayia Triadha, and you can see some

15 A gypsum stand for a double axe set on a pole, a royal and sacred object to protect the contents of the Storerooms. Double axes can also be seen cut on the gypsum orthostat wall of the Storeroom behind, and the marks of the fire that burnt Knossos down in about 1375. In Storeroom 7 inside you can see cists, or boxes set in the floor, and part of a buttress to support a column base and column on the floor above.

from Tylissos reconstructed in the Heraklion Museum. The presence of so many double axes emphasizes how important the corn and wine and oil and wool and cloth, and the other goods stored in the stone cists set in the floor were for the rulers of Knossos. They guarded these possessions with their royal and sacred symbol, the double axe. But, though the double axes may have deterred pilferers, there was little to protect the goods from catching fire. When the palace burnt down in about 1375 the heat was so intense here that several of the orthostats still have thick black fire marks, as they do on the outside of the palace in this same area by the West Porch 3 (Plate 10).

You will also notice from your viewpoint that the entrances of Storerooms 4 and 5 have been narrowed some time after they were built. I am not sure why. Perhaps, as with the buttresses built in 7 and 9, this was intended to support something on the upper floor; or more probably it was designed for restricting access to these rooms.

The rest of the upper storey is more complicated to reconstruct. The large staircase to the South of the Throne Room 18 was built over cists of Middle Minoan III date (which you can see now through grilles): therefore the staircase belongs to Late Minoan I at least, or maybe even later in the life of the New Palace. Column bases in the centre of this staircase either supported a roof or another flight of stairs up to a second floor. To the South of the stairs (on the left as you look from the Central Court) Evans conjectured that there was a large hall with three columns and a smaller treasury containing ritual vases. These vases were found tumbled down into the debris below. Much of this area then, from the Throne Room right along the West side of the Central Court (Plate 11), seems to have been devoted to religion, and to the storing of presents offered in the name of religion or majesty.

If you leave the upper floor Tricolumnar Hall, as Evans called it, by its South exit, you come into an anteroom which opens into the Propylon 19 at the top of Staircase 20. We have now reached from inside what was the ceremonial entrance to these large halls which we have just been reconstructing above the West side of the palace. I hope it will not disturb you that we have come this way round: many tours bring one immediately up the Staircase but, since so much of the Corridor of the Procession Fresco has fallen away on the South side of the palace (p. 54), it is impossible to reach this grand ceremonial entrance from the West Porch without suddenly leaping over the ruins of a wall which was originally impassable. I think you lose some of the impact of Knossos if you break in like a thief in the night. You need time to enjoy Knossos and to grow familiar with how it might have been originally.

The evidence for the Staircase is puzzling, and most of what you see today has been restored. Where the steps are now, the excavators found a blank area containing a mass of clay which they called the 'Central Clay Area'. Then they realised that the clay must have been the foundation of what would have been a staircase (because of the change in level), to connect the imposing Propylaea 21 to the South of the 'Clay Area' with the equally grand rooms which they knew to be on the first floor (Evans's *piano nobile*). The Minoans accordingly had planned this link in a grand manner: it would have been striking if one had come, as they intended, along the relatively narrow Corridor of the Procession

16 The Lobby of the Stone Seat **22** (the seat is on the right) with the reconstructed entrance to the Pillar Crypts **25** behind. To the left is the entrance to a passage that bypasses the Crypts. The wall on the right is made of gypsum slabs for wall facing, stacked horizontally.

Fresco **4** from the West Court, accompanied into the palace by the people in the fresco bringing gifts, turned the corner and soon suddenly entered a light well on one's left and so come into the large, high porch of the Propylaea to go up the Staircase. Note how wide the column and pillar bases are, and how large are the door jambs and the sockets for the door posts. It was designed to impress. Part of it has been reconstructed in the grand way, not unfairly; and copies of the Procession Fresco have been put up on the wall. A carved stone frieze ran above the columns.

Let us leave the Proplyaea and return to the Central Court, to finish our tour of the West side. If you stand back for a moment in the middle of the Court, you see a varied facade (Plate 11) before you which divides into three blocks. At the North end is the Throne Room suite, at the South the pillars of a verandah – which is similar to the verandahs on the East sides of the Central Courts of Phaistos and Mallia – and in the middle steps lead down into the central block which we shall visit now to see the places where many of the palace's sacred treasures were kept. To the North of these steps is the small Tripartite or Columnar Shrine, two sets of two columns flanking a central column at a higher level behind which was the inner sanctuary of the shrine. We walk down the five steps into the Lobby of the Stone Seat **22** (Plates 16, 17), which has a similarly patterned floor to those in the Throne Room and its Anteroom. The walls of the Lobby are unusual – layers of thin gypsum slabs laid horizontally like bricks. The slabs were used throughout the palace as a facing for walls: those here may have been surplus.

To the South (to the left) of the Lobby of the Stone Seat are the remains of a

17 Part of the Lobby of the Stone Seat **22** and the Pillar Crypts **25** as they were found.

small paved room where the excavators found the ritual vessels of the Central Treasury tumbled down from the collapsed floor above. North of the Lobby are two small storerooms. The Room of the Tall Pithos **23** – you will see why it has this name – is the first of these. It has a gypsum-lined cist set in the floor, and there are gaps in its South wall which might have been for shelves. The second room is known after the two large containers sunk in the floor which Evans called the Temple Repositories **24** (Plate 18), 'Temple' from the sacred nature of their contents, 'Repositories' perhaps because these goods were put away for ever here once the containers had been covered over by the floor. Two other smaller boxes were in due course set in that floor during Late Minoan I. One of these later cists can still be seen in the floor between the two Repository containers; the other was above the West Repository, and was removed when it was excavated. When the area was first dug there was nothing in the floor to show that these earlier Repositories existed, but within two years it was seen to be sagging, which led to their discovery. These stores date from Middle Minoan IIIB. Another store below the grille in the Staircase **18** immediately to the North belongs with them.

The later cist which lies between the two Repositories is shallow and fitted for a cover, which could have been of wood or gypsum. This cist is of the same type as those which were built during the life of the New Palace in the floor of the Long Corridor of the Storeroom and in the Storerooms themselves. The two Repositories however are quite different. The East one (nearer the Central Court) is built of dovetailed slabs, while the West one is of massive blocks, a single block running the whole length of each side. Red clay has been packed in

18   The Temple Repositories **24** of Middle Minoan IIIB date (1600–1550) with a
later cist between them. The East Repository in the foreground contained the famous
Snake Goddess.

between the courses to make a tight fit, and you will notice pegholes in the sides which would have supported a wooden framework of shelves. In the East Repository the famous faience figures of a Snake Goddess were found, and with them faience vases, floral sprays, crosses and shells, and heaps of painted sea shells which decorated the floor and ledges on which the cult objects were put. Many clay vases were found as well, which could have held wine, water and oil used in the ceremonies: the most exotic are a group of large bellied jugs with pulled back spouts, decorated with strange birds with big circular bellies. These jugs were made in the Cyclades, possibly in Melos, and are of a quite different clay, shape and style of decoration from contemporary Cretan jugs. In the West Repository Evans found plenty of gold foil, but it looked to him as if the richest contents had been robbed: he thought its elaborate, tight construction must have been intended to protect a gold treasure which could have been even more valuable than the faience Goddesses.

Return to the Lobby of the Stone Seat and turn West (right) through the central door into two rooms with central pillars, the Pillar Crypts **25** (Plates 16, 17). The pillars of each are engraved with double axes. Either side of the pillar in the East Crypt (the Crypt nearer the Central Court) are shallow stone trays set in the floor: these have also been called cists by archaeologists but, though they look like the cists for storage or boxes which we have seen in the floors of the storerooms, their function was probably quite different. They probably held sacred offerings or liquids. In the West Crypt there is a bench, and in a storeroom off the East Crypt a row of similar stone trays along the East and North walls which have given it the name of the Vat Room **26**. It was here that Evans found a small treasure dating to Middle Minoan IA, the phase immediately before the palace was begun, which he took as an indication of the continuing sanctity of this area, since the votive character of this deposit is like that of the Temple Repositories buried the other side of the wall some three hundred years later. It may be that the Vat Room treasure was offered as a foundation deposit, an offering made when the palace was built to ensure its prosperity. In the storeroom beside the Vat Room, now closed off, is a stone bench which may have been a stand for pithoi.

These Pillar Crypts are dark rooms and you may want to hurry through. But they are important and deserve a few moments' pause. What are they there for? There is a clue at Mallia, which has a Pillar Crypt in much the same position, on the West side of the Central Court and, as at Knossos, connected to shrines and sacred treasuries. The Pillar Crypts of both places seem then connected with offerings and with religion – probably a chthonic cult of the earth and its fruitfulness. At Knossos they are next to the Temple Repositories on one side and to the Storerooms on the other which are engraved with the same double axes. People could have waited in the Lobby of the Stone Seat to perform rituals, that may have been private, in the Crypts. If they had no business in the Crypts, there is another exit from the Lobby of the Stone Seat (the left exit in Plate 16) which goes into a passage which bypasses the Crypts and takes one more directly to the Long Corridor of the Storerooms. One would conclude that the Crypts at Knossos and the Crypt at Mallia were used for ceremonies which involved offerings, of probably both farm produce and the

19   Storeroom 9 with a complement of cists and *pithoi* (storage jars). The buttress on the left is the pair of that in Plate 15.

work of craftsmen, and perhaps rituals with light – as the rooms are so dark.

You leave the Pillar Crypts by the door at the South-West corner and, passing the passage that comes direct from the Lobby of the Stone Seat bypassing the Crypts, and a long narrow space and a passage next to it which must have held a staircase and its return, you come to the Long Corridor of the Storerooms **27**, now fenced off, which we have already noticed from the upper floor.

This Long Corridor is one of the most impressive parts of the palace. Its length, the row of Storerooms off it, and the way that every space is used (even as far as putting cists below the flagstones), are not just careful architecture but are also important evidence of the wealth of Knossos and of its economic base which enabled it to afford luxuries and splendour. The administration of the levies that allowed so much activity, and some of the activities themselves, are recorded in the Linear B tablets most of which were found in the rooms in the area of **14** and **15** by the North end of the Corridor. Doubtless there were similar things recorded in the Linear A and Hieroglyphic texts that preceded them, which are of course still undeciphered.

Most of the details of the Storerooms (Plate 19) were pointed out when we stood on the upper floor: cists in the floor, double axe stands, marks of burning and the layout of the Storerooms. Down at ground level you can appreciate how much wood was used in the building from the many timber holes preserved. Other details to notice if you should happen to be allowed in: Storeroom 8, where as many cists have been fitted in as possible – there is even one aligned North-South below the threshold and another like it in 7 – showing how valuable space was; frescoes still in position in 12; opposite 14 a staircase leading up to the first floor; 14 to 17 were blocked off some time, as you can get into them only if you go through 17; and 18 would have been reached from the upper floor as there is no direct way into it, which makes it certain that there was a staircase here in the North-West corner of the palace.

You can reach the North end of the Long Corridor of the Storerooms from the Corridor of the Stone Basin past the North Storerooms of the Old Palace and past the spot where the Hieroglyphic tablets of the Old Palace were found stored under the stairs in the Long Corridor.

The East Side

The East side of the Palace offers little to see from the Central Court since it is built into the slope of the hill. One can however reconstruct one large hall at the level of the Court, roughly marked by the slab of concrete jutting out over the East side to the North of the Grand Staircase, and there were doubtless others. Below, the reconstructed rooms give a fair idea of how this part of the Palace would have been, since the height of two of the upper floor levels is preserved by the flights of the Grand Staircase **28**. Apart from its grand rooms, this area (Fig. 7) has interesting small rooms and passages and abounds in architectural details which make it the most instructive part of the palace for understanding Minoan architecture; and since two floors are preserved into the side of the hill, much of the building has not fallen down or has moved only a little, which allows us to be more confident in reconstructing the original appearance.

The Grand Staircase **28** (Plate 20) is particularly well preserved, pressed as it is against the edge of the cutting (and now roofed). Four flights of gentle steps and broad landings can be seen, and the beginning of a fifth. You have a fine view of them from the Hall of the Colonnades at the bottom or from the Upper Hall of the Royal Guard on the first floor down. They appear astonishingly light and graceful. The architect's detail which may be the clue to this illusion is that the space between the balustrade of the stair and the bottom of the flight above stays constant, as the balustrade steps down in parallel with what is above, and the columns keep the same height throughout. The effect is of light, but firm, control.

On the first floor down, you come to the Upper Hall of the Royal Guard which opens onto the light well around the stairs. Evans has restored full size figure-of-eight shields of oxhide stretched on a frame, in imitation of those which he thought were placed on the walls in the equivalent room below.

20 The top of the Grand Staircase **28** on the East side of Knossos, as found by Evans. The Staircase had bulged where it had originally been open.

Beyond the Upper Hall are conjectural rooms restored on the roof over the Hall of the Double Axes below.

If you do not turn into the Upper Hall of the Royal Guard but continue straight ahead from the Grand Staircase at this level, you come into the Corridor of the Bays **29**, which has three large piers with spaces, or bays, between them. These piers must have supported the floor of the hall above, where we remarked that the big concrete slab is now, and – as with the piers in the West Storerooms – we can confidently restore columns or pillars at the entrance to the hall or perhaps its anteroom. It could have been a two-room arrangement, as in the Throne Room the opposite side of the Central Court. Next to the Corridor of the Bays is the Storeroom of the Medallion Pithoi **30**, named after the large storage jars with their relief medallions. These two rooms

belong to the first phase of the New Palace, and so does the conjectural Hall above them. There had probably been a similar storage space there earlier as, where the pavement of the Storeroom of the Medallion Pithoi has been broken away, you will see the floor of the Old Palace period below with a circular stand in the floor for storage jars. The present arrangement of the Corridor of the Bays and the Storeroom did not survive longer than the end of Middle Minoan III, as the rooms were filled up with rubble and the door to the Grand Staircase blocked off, apparently so that the floor of the Hall above could be raised: thus in its later phase one walked up the steps of a three-columned portico (the columns were over the piers) and into the Hall. This arrangement complemented the porticoed buildings, especially the Tripartite Shrine, on the opposite side of the Central Court.

The part to the North of the Corridor of the Bays is difficult to understand

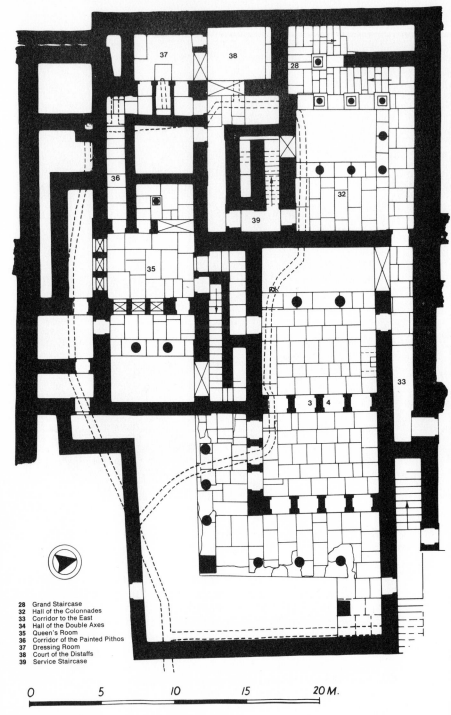

28 Grand Staircase
32 Hall of the Colonnades
33 Corridor to the East
34 Hall of the Double Axes
35 Queen's Room
36 Corridor of the Painted Pithos
37 Dressing Room
38 Court of the Distaffs
39 Service Staircase

0   5   10   15   20 M.

Fig. 7.   Plan of the 'Domestic Quarter' of Knossos.

76

21   The Corridor to the East **33** (East-West Corridor) leads from the foot of the Grand Staircase **28** to the Hall of the Double Axes **34** through the door on the right (the window opens onto the Hall's light well), and at the end to the left to the East Portico **40** and other rooms in the North-East part of the palace.

since so much has fallen down the hill. What is visible belongs both to the Old and to the New Palaces. There are a number of storerooms and several enclosed spaces, which are between the supports of the East Hall and other rooms above. A large hollowed slab and drain in the room next to the Storeroom of the Medallion Pithoi may have carried the rain away from a light well which was part of the Hall complex.

A little further North you come into the Corridor of the Draughtboard **31** – the Minoan draughtboard in the Heraklion Museum was found here. Below a grille you see the fresh water supply system: terracotta pipes of a tapering shape designed so that the flow of water would create a head and prevent sediments' collecting. Each pipe has a collar to fit the next.

From the Corridor of the Draughtboard you can reach the North-East Hall **45** and the North-East Storerooms **46**. You will notice the Storeroom of the Giant Pithoi **44** off to your right, but it is probably more convenient to visit this and the East Bastion **47** after you have been to what were probably the royal apartments.

Return to the Grand Staircase and go down to the second floor. You come to what I find the most interesting part of Knossos because it is the most complex and also the most integrated group of rooms in Minoan Crete (Fig. 7). You will notice that the units of this 'Domestic Quarter', as Evans called it, are at the same time isolated and interconnecting, with dark passages between them which give privacy and coolness; that there are also three light wells and one light area in the Quarter which again ensure privacy, light and natural circulation of the air; that there are thick walls with rows of double doors, permitting the rooms to be open or shut or partly open or shut; and finally that the style of this part of the building is sturdy, but still quite delicate. The methods of tackling the problems of the fierce heat and light are similar to those used in Greece today. Physical conditions of course have changed little.

The Hall of the Colonnades **32** is at the bottom of the Grand Staircase. An outer room and therefore probably more public, it corresponds to the Upper Hall of the Royal Guard. One could leave it either to go through narrow passages to the Dressing Room **37** and on to the Queen's Room **35**, or take the East-West Corridor **33** off to the East (Plate 21). This Corridor would have been shut by a door. It leads eventually to an area of workshops. If you go through the door, immediately to the right is a window opening on to the light well in the Hall of the Double Axes **34** and next to the window is the entrance to the Hall.

The Hall of the Double Axes **34** was probably the ruler's room where he slept and dispensed justice and performed other duties and pleasures. It is a double room, with a large light well at its West end and a deep verandah on the East and South-East (Plate 22): air would have come from the verandah through the Room and ascended in the thermal which the Light Well creates. The Light Well is of fine ashlar masonry, with a double axe carved on each block – proof that these rooms were as royal as were the Storerooms on the other side of the Central Court crammed with the palace's wealth. From the West half of the Hall a dogleg corridor leads to the Queen's Room **35** (see plan, Fig. 7), but you can also reach it by taking a more direct corridor from the East half of the Hall, or by walking round from the verandah to reach the outside of the light well of

22 The counterplay of piers and columns in the Hall of the Double Axes **34** at Knossos, as seen from its verandah. At the back is the Hall's light well, each block of which is engraved with a double axe.

the Queen's Room. Opposite these passages, on the North wall of the Hall is a plaster construction, which may be the remnants of the throne on which 'Minos' really sat (for the throne of the Throne Room see p. 63); and another throne has been restored in the East half. The Hall of the Double Axes is a cool and pleasant room, and ideal for the Cretan climate. It is large, but not oppressive. As you walk around, notice particularly the interplay of the columns and piers. It could not be more delightful.

The Queen's Room **35** can be reached by four ways, as I have said: the dogleg corridor, the outside route, the way through its Dressing Room from the Hall of the Double Axes, and by the stairs down from the floor above – a proper setting for palace intrigues. It is lit by light wells to the South and East. I imagine there may have been a small garden in the East light well, to solace the Queen (or the High Priestess) and her ladies. The Room has been restored to look feminine and attractive with its benches and windows and the Dancing Girl and Dolphin frescoes which sometime adorned it: a Minoan boudoir. It also has plenty of evidence of two periods of building, both being within the life of the New Palace: thus there are two floor levels visible in the Room and in the porch of the East light well, and two formal frescoes, an earlier with spirals and a later with rosettes. The Dolphin Fresco, now shown inside the room, was actually found in the East light well, and had probably originally been on the far wall of the light well. It would have been an attractive *trompe l'oeil*. The fresco probably belongs to the last phase of the New Palace, although these motifs had been popular from the beginning of the period in Middle Minoan III, and similar dolphins of that time were painted on frescoes in Melos. The Dancing Girl, whose long twists of black hair stream out as she whirls, was also found in the light well.

In the opposite corner is the Bathroom, here on the same level as the rest of the rooms. It is enclosed by a half-wall, like a modern bar or room-divider, which probably had a curtain above. The clay tub you see in it was found in pieces in the entrance and in the main room, scattered when the Bathroom became a lime dump some time after the palace was destroyed. The fluted column is modelled on one in a bathroom in the Little Palace (p. 91).

Leave the Queen's Room by the Corridor of the Painted Pithos **36** (the pithos has been removed) and you come to the Dressing Room **37**. In its South-West corner is a low platform which supported a divan and heaps of cushions – there is another such in the room off the main room at Ayia Triadha. Opposite is its private light well, named the Court of the Distaffs **38**, which may have also been planted with flowers. The feature here that many visitors study with care is the Lavatory, which blocks the corridor at the East end of the room. It is a small room shut off by partition walls of thin double gypsum slabs, in which a groove would have held the seat. The seat was placed over the large drain at the end. Outside the Lavatory in the Dressing Room is a stone slab slightly hollowed with a hole in it, which leads to the drain below the seat. Fresh water would have been poured down this small hole to flush the Lavatory. One can still find this type of lavatory in use in Crete today.

If you continue, you come into another passage in the floor of which you can see the water system, by which fresh water was supplied and dirty water (from the Lavatory) removed. Passing a locked room on your right which may originally have been a treasury as it is so secret (clay sealings were found in it fallen from an archive room above) you turn a corner and come to the foot of a small service staircase **39**. In the area below its return the famous ivory acrobat was found in what was probably a cupboard. The service staircase leads to a concrete floor restored over the rooms you have just been visiting.

The North-East Quarter

To reach the North-East parts of the palace, proceed to the Hall of the Colonnades and turn right, as if you were returning to the Hall of the Double Axes, but continue along the Corridor and turn left at the top of the stairs leading down at the end of the corridor. You can enter another corridor, and can turn right to a room called the Lobby of the Wooden Posts and through it enter the East Portico **40**. The East Portico is a verandah which overlooks the hill of Ailias on the opposite side of the Kairatos valley where many of the Minoans of Knossos were buried. The flat land at the bottom of the valley is where Evans thought the bull games took place. If you do not visit the East Portico as you walk along the Corridor you will see in a fenced off room to the right **41**, lumps of green stone, some of them sawn. This dark green stone with lighter green phenocrysts is Spartan basalt, or *lapis lacedaemonius*, which crops out in the Peloponnese near Sparta. It is a rare stone in the Bronze Age, not used before Late Minoan I though the Romans used it as wall panelling and in floors. Above this storeroom was probably a stone vase maker's workshop, as two unfinished amphoras of gypsum were found fallen down from it.

The corridor leads to the 'School Room' **42**, so called because of the benches round three of its sides. But the plaster containers by them suggest that it was not for children but rather for craftsmen who could have put their raw materials in these containers. In fact it seems quite likely that the whole of this part of the palace was used for craftsmen and for storing their products and materials.

Next to the School Room is the Court of the Stone Spout **43** where the water channelled from the gutters of the (inferred) East Hall – represented by the slab of concrete at the level of the Central Court (p. 73) – came through a stone spout in the West wall and was led to the brick well below a grille to the North of the restored wall. This system was connected with the hollowed slab and drain which you may have seen in the room next to the Storeroom of the Medallion Pithoi (p. 74: **30**). A verandah leads off from this small Court, through which you come to the stairs going down to the East Bastion. Ahead of you are the Giant Pithoi of the Old Palace period, and behind this to the North were rooms where the fine Old Palace Kamares was kept. Up the hill to the West (left) of the Storeroom of the Giant Pithoi **44** is a row of openings with grooves which may have been part of pens for animals **47**. At the foot of the staircase is the East Bastion **48**, an exit from the palace and a way of reaching the bull games if they were held on the flat ground below, and of coming to the Royal Villa (p. 87) and other houses in the Minoan town which have still to be excavated.

The East Bastion (Plate 23) is a well defended postern gate. Its most interesting feature is the drainage system for storm water. As you will see, the drain descends in a curved runnel designed to precipitate the water into small settling basins. In these the mud fell to the bottom, and could easily be scooped out, while the water flowed on in another runnel to the next basin. In Crete when the rain comes, it falls very heavily and washes down masses of debris which clogs the drains: these basins are a practical and an imaginative solution of this problem.

You can return now from the East Bastion the way you came and up the Grand Staircase, which appears an even more distinguished piece of architecture than when you walk down it.

The South-East Quarter

At the top of the Grand Staircase, turn left (towards the South, the hill of Gypsades in the foreground and, further away, Mount Iouktas on which was a peak shrine), and walk along the Central Court and down a ramp at its South-East corner. You will come to a doorway on your left which opens out on to a staircase. The staircase was the way from the South Entrance through the South-East quarter to the East rooms we have just visited. Beside it to the South (on your right) is a light well.

Turn left at the foot of the stairs to enter the Corridor of the Sword Tablets **49** and what is left of the South-East quarter. This part of the palace suffered from the earthquakes at the end of Middle Minoan III – you can see more of the

23 The East Bastion **48** is a way down from the palace to the flat ground in the
bottom of the Kairatos valley, where Evans thought that the bull games took place.
The drain with its settling pools comes down beside the steps of the Bastion.

devastation of that time in the House of the Sacred Oxen and the House of the Fallen Blocks a few metres away (p. 84) – but it seems to have been cleared out and in use at the time of the great disaster of Knossos c.1375, and then again cleared out and used when the ruins were reoccupied in the thirteenth century.

Now take the first small passage to your right and you will see the Shrine of the Double Axes **50**. This is one of the most interesting of the domestic shrines of Minoan buildings, found as it had been left in the thirteenth century. The Shrine consists of a small room with a plastered bench at the back. On the bench and on the floor beach pebbles were strewn: resting on the bench were two plaster horns of consecration, and some clay figurines of which the largest was probably the Minoan Goddess. A round plaster offering table was set below in the pebbles of the floor; and on the floor were jars and bowls which contained the foods and goods offered in the Shrine.

After looking at the Shrine, continue along the short passage till you can turn left and walk along to reach two rooms which were not cleared after the earthquake at the end of Middle Minoan III. They lie off the Passage of the Lily Jars **51**, so called after the vases with lilies painted white. In one of the rooms is a clay bath, in the other three large storage jars.

Return the way you came to leave this part of the palace, and continue down the ramp until you either turn left (East) to reach the Middle Minoan III houses or right (West) to see what is left of the South front of the Palace.

The South Front

The South front is badly preserved. You see principally the remains of terraces and thick piers which formed the substructure of the building. You will notice also a restored large horns of consecration – its size is comparable to that of the broken original by the Theatral Area – and Evans's restoration at the end of the Corridor of the Procession Fresco where it reaches the Central Court, with the so-called Priest King Fresco which has been discussed (p. 54).

Below the terrace is the South Entrance **52** at the East end, and the South House (p. 85) preserved in a deep cutting at the West. Between them are remains of Neolithic and Early Minoan houses.

At the West end of the South Corridor you can turn left to walk down the Minoan road that comes from the other side of the little valley and see the South House. Or you can turn right, climb a modern stone staircase and reach the Corridor of the Procession Fresco leading to the West Court where the tour of the palace began.

Houses around Knossos

Around the palace of Knossos was the large Minoan city, little of which has been excavated: apart from digging the palace, the archaeologists of Knossos have busied themselves more with where the Minoan inhabitants were buried than where they lived. Of the houses that we know most are grand, well built town houses and are comparable to the grand, well built country houses we shall be discussing below. They were presumably occupied by nobility, perhaps when they came to pay their respects at court. Or minor royalty could have lived in them, or rich merchants, if that class had a separate identity in Minoan Crete.

There are two groups of houses to see, those immediately around the palace and those which are further away. We shall look at those close to the palace first, and start on the South front where the tour of the palace has ended. Several houses are preserved at the South-East corner of the palace.

Around the Palace

House of the Sacrificed Oxen   53
House of the Fallen Blocks   54
House of the Chancel Screen   55
South-East House   56

The first houses at the South-East corner of the palace are the House of the Sacrificed Oxen **53** and the House of the Fallen Blocks **54**. They were built, with the New Palace, in Middle Minoan III and were destroyed by the earthquake towards the end of that phase, and never rebuilt. They are both quite well constructed, but they are not of ashlar. Neither has any apparent entrance, which must mean that only the basements are preserved. The rest of their buildings were knocked down by the earthquake, which was strong enough to send the huge blocks of the South front of the palace crashing into the second houses, where they still are today. The first house was named after the two heads of sacrificed oxen that were found in the South-East and North-West corners of its Southern basement. They were set in the ground with portable altars in front of them, and may have been intended to propitiate the deity of earthquakes, whose delight is in the roaring of bulls, according to the *Iliad* (20.405ff.) of some nine hundred years later.

The House of the Chancel Screen **55** beyond these two houses has been partly covered in, but you can see the screen, which is its most interesting feature. It is at the back of the main room and has two columns, with a door and a platform behind on which is a seat or altar. The triple arrangement of the space is like that of the Tripartite Shrine on the West side of the Central Court, and that of the Shrine in the house at Vathypetro; but the Royal Villa has the most similar screen, as you will see. Both screens must be connected with religion, though we do not know exactly how they were used. When the house was dug, the workmen christened it the Priest's House.

The South-East House **56** below is of much the same size, but more has been left open to view. A well built house with plenty of gypsum and of ashlar masonry, it is set on a slightly more easterly alignment than the House of the Chancel Screen. This may have been done to accommodate its position lower down the slope.

You enter the South-East House down a double flight of stairs into a corridor, which may lead to another possible entrance from the East. Next to the stairs at the North end of the house is a pillar room, with a cist in the floor, two double axe stands and a niche in the East wall. This arrangement is of course similar to what we have seen in the West side of the palace. The niche may have been for offerings and not for a light since a tall purple stone lamp was found in the room. From this room you can go South into the main room which has excellent ashlar masonry and a gypsum floor, and an interior division wall of gypsum slabs on end. This room was lit mainly from a small peristyle court (that is, a court you could walk around under cover) to the South, which could be shut off by doors. The crazy paving in the middle was open to the sky, while the floor of the cloistered area is of gypsum. To the West another room opened on to the court, and could also be shut by doors.

House of the Monolithic Pillars 57

Further to the North on the East side of the palace are some buildings that are probably contemporary with the Old Palace, a potter's kiln, the East facade of the palace itself, and a room of the House of the Monolithic Pillars which is earlier (Middle Minoan IA). The house is named after the two tall gypsum pillars which unusually are of all one piece. They are in a basement which has four bays at the back, separated by three piers, an arrangement like that in the Corridor of the Bays inside the Palace nearby.

South House 58

By the South-West corner of the palace is the South House. It is set in a large cutting, which removed Neolithic and Early Minoan II and III houses, some of which are still visible below the South Front of the palace. To the West a road runs down to the Viaduct and the Caravanserai, the little building you can see across the valley. It is a pleasant setting above the streams looking out on the hill of Gypsades and Mount Iouktas, but it is very hot in summer. The House has been restored so that one can visit three levels. Its back wall has been preserved by the cutting up to eight courses high.

You enter the South House from the road to its West (one of the main Minoan approaches to the palace) down through the reconstructed upper floor into a pillar room with a double axe stand and a stand for sacred offerings and go through into a North-South passage. At its North end is a bath off a hall in the North-East corner of the house: the hall has a central crazy pavement bordered by gypsum flagstones. In the East wall of the hall is a window, which looks out over the house's yard or garden on to the retaining wall built against the Early Minoan houses to shore up the cutting. To the South, doors open on to a forehall and through it to the vestibule and main entrance which are at the South-East corner of the House. If you return to the passage, stairs go down to the basement floor into a pillar room with three pillars.

House of the Frescoes 59

If you return from the South House, up the modern flight of steps, and along the Corridor of the Procession Fresco, you will come back to the West Court. There are still some other houses around the palace you can see, but they are not as spectacular as those on the South side. Immediately South of the West Court are some indeterminate remains, including pillar basements; on the opposite side of the West Court, in the area between the *koulouras* and the Theatral Area is the North-West Treasure House, where a store of bronze equipment was found. There is little to see of it now. Further on, the Royal Road **7**, we have already said, was lined with buildings: some, mostly basements, can be seen a little way down it on the left, that is on the South. Behind these basements is the House of the Frescoes **59**, another rich house of the earlier part of the period of the New Palaces, which has produced some very fine naturalistic frescoes, including the Blue Monkey and the Blue Birds, perhaps pigeons or doves, in a rocky landscape, and many flower designs. Painted Linear A inscriptions were found also on the frescoes – Evans was reminded of texts from the Koran on the walls of mosques.

North-East House

On the East side, some storerooms by the North-East corner of the palace are all that remains of the North-East House. It lies on the way to the Royal Villa (see below).

Outside the Palace

We shall start again on the South with the Caravanserai, and then go North to the Royal Villa and the Little Palace and the so-called Unexplored Mansion.

Keys for the Royal Villa and the Little Palace, and for the Temple Tomb, should be obtained from the guardian's office at the entrance to the palace.

Caravanserai
House of the High Priest

To come to the Caravanserai, take the modern road up the valley from the palace entrance and about 100 m. after the bridge a path leads down to it on the left. The Caravanserai looks out on to the palace: the view alone justifies the walk. Its main room, which is like a porch, was decorated with the famous Partridge Fresco, which is in the same style as the frescoes of the House of the Frescoes. In the next room are the remains of a footbath, fed by the springs that crop out here. Below, and to the West of, the footbath is a Spring Chamber: it has a small pool in the floor, with ledges or benches around and a central niche which may have held a lamp. The Spring Chamber was found filled with pottery, ashes, and offerings of the last years of the Minoan era (1100 or later), when a cult was practised here, perhaps one of water and, one would like to think, of ancestors.

Further down below the Caravanserai the path comes to the four massive piers of the Viaduct, with steps between them down to the stream. These piers would have supported a wooden bridge across the stream, which the traveller would have crossed to reach the palace after refreshing himself at the Caravanserai.

If you return to the road and continue walking a few minutes up the valley, you come to the House of the High Priest (marked by a faded sign) just below the road. There is little to see, but it has a screen somewhat similar to that in the Royal Villa. A little beyond the House of the High Priest is the Temple Tomb, a built royal tomb of the New Palace period. It is on two levels and has two pillar basements on the lower. Its masonry is extremely well preserved. The Temple Tomb is worth visiting.

Royal Villa

For the Royal Villa, walk up the village street of Knossos and take the road down to the right opposite the last cafe (just beyond where the street crosses Royal Road) to the village of Makrytikhos. In the village turn right and take the path leading up the Kairatos valley on its West side. You will come to the Royal Villa on the left before you reach the palace area.

Like the East side of Knossos and like the palace of Ayia Triadha, the Royal Villa is built into a cutting and faces East. It lies only a little way above the stream, and would have been very pleasant, with a garden that probably ran down to the water. It is generously planned, and plenty of gypsum was used in the building.

You see now a hall and a forehall, which perhaps faced on to a light well. Behind is a chancel screen with a central recess for a seat or stand: this narrow room was lit from a light well, which would have shown up dramatically a person or a statue there. To the South is another light well, from which one can reach the hall by a door below the stairs; but, as there are now no important rooms lit by this light well, its main purpose must have been to light rooms on the floor above. The main entrance was presumably on this upper level; stairs lead up at the South-West corner – there may even have been a third storey. In the room in the South-East corner, notice a double gypsum partition wall, like that in the Queen's Lavatory inside the palace. At the North end of the Royal Villa is a pillar crypt, with cists for offerings either side of the pillars, an arrangement we shall find more examples of in the Little Palace. The sockets of the ceiling beams were found in the excavation. Evans estimated that tree trunks were used of a width of over 0.80 m.

Little Palace
'Unexplored Mansion'

For the Little Palace, you will find a gate in the wall on the left about 15 m. from the last cafe in Knossos village as you walk up the hill towards Heraklion. Ask for the key first at the entrance of the palace.

The Little Palace is the largest town house. Like the Royal Villa, it faces East and is built into the cutting. It would have been extremely hot here on summer mornings, unless it was shaded by trees; but the shadows from the Acropolis hills behind come early in the afternoon and make this side of the valley particularly pleasant at the end of the day. Since the Little Palace is built into a cutting, its walls have been preserved to a greater height than usual, as they are at the South House, which is also in a cutting. Of the main stairs one and a half flights are still standing and can be seen in the shed in the centre of the site, but the ground level slopes away quickly, and the principal rooms are badly preserved and a considerable part of their ground plan reconstructed (Fig. 9).

These main rooms are surprisingly large, larger even than the Hall of the Double Axes in the palace, with rows of columns and piers which have now rotted away. The main room is a double one, with floors like those in the palace,

Fig. 8. Plan of the Palace of Phaistos.

25 Storeroom office (?)
26 Corridor of the Storerooms
27–37 Storerooms
48 North Court
49 Garden (?)
63–64 East Wing
63 Main room
64 Peristyle hall
66 Grand Staircase
69a Light well
70 Guardroom
74 Peristyle Hall
77–79 Tripartite room
78 Light well
83 Bath
103 Peristyle

Lavatory

Fetish Shrine

Hall of the Peristyle

0   5   10M

Fig. 9.   Plan of the Little Palace of Knossos.

of crazy paving surrounded by gypsum flagstones. The third room, the Hall of the Peristyle, is very similar to the Peristyle Hall at Phaistos, which we shall be discussing shortly. To the West off the North half-room is a lavatory, and to the East a small porch with crazy paving, which was probably a verandah where one could sit and look across the valley. The verandah continues outside the South half-room, and perhaps outside the Hall of the Peristyle also.

The smaller shed on the site covers the Fetish Shrine, originally a bath which was converted after the great destruction of Knossos into a shrine when stones of rude shape were placed on the balustrade. The spaces between the wooden columns on the small parapet were blocked up, and the impressions of the columns have been preserved. They were found to be fluted, with fifteen flutings.

At the South end of the Little Palace are a number of pillar basements. One is in the South-West corner, and cult objects were found fallen down into a shaft beside it. They had come from a shrine or sacred treasury above, and included a double axe stand and the famous bull's head rhyton (on display in the Heraklion Museum: similar rhytons have been found at Zakro and Mycenae, and they are shown on the Keftiu paintings in Egypt and in the Linear B tablets (Plate 9)). At the South-East corner are two other pillar basements or crypts, which you can reach by a staircase. That on the East has three pillars and two cists – the cists have a central hole, perhaps to hold a banner, or a standard, or a double axe on a pole. That on the West has pillars either side of a cist.

Many mud bricks were found in the Little Palace, measuring 0.45 × 0.45 × 0.12 m. Tall pieces of gypsum were also used as door jambs.

Behind the Little Palace are parts of two more grand town houses which are still being excavated. The one on the South was called the 'Unexplored Mansion' by Evans who identified it but was not able to dig it. You notice splendid ashlar facades, and an indent for a window in the East facade of the 'Unexplored Mansion'. Inside it are rooms with cists with central holes, and corridors, storerooms and the remains of a staircase. The East-West passage near the South end of the building was reached by a bridge from the Little Palace. In the middle is a room that is of great importance for the history of Minoan Crete: a square room faced with ashlar with four pillars, of surprising elegance and obviously the ground floor of another fine room above – a little of the walling of the upper floor was found in position during the excavation, and has been preserved. What is odd is that in this pillar hall there are several rough and scrappy walls, as if people came and camped, or squatted, who had no idea of how to live in such grand surroundings. Their only interest was to define a small area as their own. Some of them worked bronze. Their nasty constructions can be dated to Late Minoan II (1450–1400) during which time there were two bad fires in the house. The house itself was begun in Late Minoan IA. Its little walls in the main room belong to the time of Mycenaean rule at Knossos and must be the work of the Mycenaeans.

6 Phaistos

Phaistos is more spectacularly situated than any other of the Minoan palaces, being built across the end of a ridge that drops into the plain of the Mesara. From Phaistos you look along the plain to the Lasithi mountains in the distance; to the South is the Asterousi range, with villages on its foothills bordering the plain as they did in Minoan times: and behind you, when you arrive and stand looking down at the palace, runs the ridge at the other end of which is the palace of Ayia Triadha, and the sea is beyond. The view to the North, best seen from the South end of the Central Court (Plate 27), is as dramatic as that along the plain. You will see that the palace is aligned towards a prominent saddle in the mountains, which are the Psiloriti or Mount Ida range. On the right of the two peaks of this saddle and a little below its summit is what appears as a large black spot, the sacred cave of Kamares which you can see from both Phaistos and Ayia Triadha. This is the mountain cave shrine which has given its name to the finest Middle Minoan pottery (such as Plate 11). It stands out most when the snow still lies on the mountains and the sun is shining and spring has arrived down below in the plain. A visit to Phaistos on a fine day in March can be a very exciting experience.

24   The West Court of the Old Palace of Phaistos with its facade. Set back above is the West facade of the New Palace, built after the Old Palace was destroyed, probably by earthquakes, at the end of Middle Minoan II. The Grand Staircase **66** of the New Palace leads to a blank-walled light well **69**, from which there are only narrow exits – the Minoan use of surprise. In the right foreground are *koulouras*, pits probably for storing grain, like those in the West Courts of Knossos and Mallia.

The architecture of the palace differs almost as much from that of Knossos as does its setting. You may already have noticed as you look down (Plate 24) that the plan seems more ordered and more simple and that you can appreciate it more quickly. From the outside it is a building dominated by a ceremonial entrance with a grand staircase leading up from the West Court. You will see as well that this flight of stairs does not come down to the level of the paved West Court, but ends about a metre higher where it is joined by another staircase coming down from an Upper Court (Plate 25), and also that there are two West facades of the palace. This is because you are looking at two different facades, the lower one belonging to the Old Palace and the higher to the New Palace. When the New Palace was built after the Old Palace had been destroyed (probably by earthquakes), the paved West Court of the Old Palace was covered with rubble a metre deep, which became the ground level of the New Palace. The New Palace was also set about 8 m. back from the Old, and this is why the facade of the Old Palace, and some of its rooms and its West Court are preserved for us. There is in fact more to see of an Old Palace at Phaistos than at the other centres, as much has been excavated since the war around the South-West corner of the palace, which was not built on in New Palace times. Unfortunately access there is restricted. It is the part under the plastic and behind the barbed wire.

The New Palace (Fig. 8. p. 88) seems to have been designed with a coherence which you will notice more quickly than was the case perhaps at Knossos. The arrangement of the building by areas and rooms is meticulous. A religious area occupies the South part of the West side, with the storerooms next to it (as at Knossos), and beyond them to the North is the Grand Staircase, the intricate and imposing approach from the West Court leading to the storerooms, the Central Court and the reception rooms which at Phaistos are mostly to the North. Right at the North end of the palace are what were presumably the private rooms, placed on the edge of the cliff for an uninterrupted view of the Psiloriti mountains. To the North-East are workshops, tucked away as they are at Knossos, and in the North part of the East side where there is still room left on the hill top, is a self-contained suite of rooms which enjoys a view quite as breathcatching as that of the rooms on the North edge. All these areas have been planned around the Central Court, as they would be in the other palaces; but at Phaistos the Central Court seems to dominate more than the other Central Courts do, partly because it is still paved, and partly from its position on the end of a hill suspended as it were between the Asterousi and the Psiloriti mountain ranges. Anybody walking in the Central Court has only to look up to see the hills beyond the buildings.

A unique architectural feature of the Central Court of Phaistos is its formal North facade, a symmetrical front with half columns, and flanking niches for sentries (Plate 27). You may be reminded of the frontal attitude of buildings in, say, Italy; you may suspect that the architect of the New Palace of Phaistos intended to enhance the view of the mountains looming up over the entrance to the probable royal apartments of the palace by contrasting the artificial formality of the one with the wildness of the other. You will feel sure, I think, as you walk around, that the New Palace is the work of one architect.

25 Staircase **6** at Phaistos leads down from the Upper Court to the foot of the Grand
Staircase **66**. The recess in the ashlar wall on the left would have held a window
above. The ground level at the foot of the stairs was taken as the base for building the
New Palace over the ruins of the Old.

When you walk down to the palace from the Tourist Pavilion, you come first to the Upper Court, which has crazy paving and a raised walk at its East end. By its West edge is a row of round holes against the retaining wall intended to hold wooden columns. The Upper Court follows but also adapts the slope of the ground, a typically Minoan treatment of the natural surroundings. Perhaps it was used as a market, the wooden columns supporting stalls. On its South side are some Minoan houses, of uncertain date; and beyond the raised walk at the East end are several slab graves, aligned to the East and possibly Christian.

To reach the West Court, go down the stairs **6** and you come into the hypothetical West Court of the New Palace which has been dug away except at the foot of the stairs where the Grand Staircase rises to the left (Plate 25). The treads of this smaller staircase coming down from the Upper Court are built up over the rock. In the sidewalls are recesses which were probably for windows.

The West Court is built on the more gently sloping side of the hill, not on the steep slope as a Classical theatre would be. A retaining wall to the North (Plate 26) holds up the Upper Court. Each course of this wall is set back a little to lessen the risk of its toppling over; and there are projections along the wall to the West, probably as this was how it could best be made to fit the contours of the hill. Below the wall and about a metre out is a line in the stones with indentations, which probably marks the position of the Old Palace period retaining wall for the Upper Court, replaced by the present retaining wall of New Palace times. If this is so, it means that the Upper Court was first laid out at the same time as the paved West Court and the facade of the Old Palace (Plate 24). The steps below the retaining wall and its predecessor are like the terraces of a stadium, and must have been intended for a crowd to watch a spectacle such as a state reception. The main raised walk leads like a red carpet down through the terraces and across the Court at an angle towards the West entrance of the Old Palace (now wired off). This walk is joined in the Court by another coming from the West, which passes a well or cistern and a *kouloura* (Plate 24). The *kouloura* is similar to those in the West Courts of Knossos and Mallia and, like them, may have held grain. If you walk to the wire, you will see others, and more of the West facade and buildings of the Old Palace still not on public view, and a road going down the hill with houses either side. Turning to the palace again, have another look at the West facades of the Old and New Palaces. The Old Palace facade has recesses for windows, as does the New Palace one above it, which confirms what you see in the Town Mosaic of Knossos, that windows came into use early. Viewed as a whole with its West Court in front, the old West facade is surprisingly monumental, a fine piece of frontal architecture.

A few rooms of the Old Palace can be seen by the foot of the Grand Staircase, where they were covered over when the level of the West Court was raised for building the New Palace. The rooms consist of a shrine **VIII** and ancillary rooms with benches, basins and receptacles for offerings. Many traces of cooking were found here, which was doubtless part of the ritual. Parts of sacrificed animals could have been cooked and eaten. Have a look also at the West entrance of the Old Palace before ascending the Grand Staircase to enter the New Palace. The main raised walk across the West Court is of crazy paving but, you will notice, when it turns to enter the Propylon (Propylon in the

26   The West Court of Phaistos belongs to the Old Palace. The terraces are similar to those of the Theatral Area at Knossos, where spectators could have watched receptions, sports or drama, or trials. The indents in the back wall probably follow the shape of the rock behind.

singular as there is only one supporting column) of the old West entrance, it changes to rectangular limestone flags and, once it is indoors, to gypsum flags. Another raised walk continues South, perhaps to a South-West entrance. If you walk up the stairs here, you will reach the level of the New Palace, where there was a minor entrance above what was the main entrance of the Old Palace. Below the modern concrete you can see some pithoi of the Old Palace still in position in their storerooms. Now return to the main entrance of the New Palace.

The Palace

The Grand Staircase **66** is the most imposing part of Phaistos, and intentionally so. Once you are on its steps, you are *in* the palace. The steps are broad and easy – no exertion to discolour the face of priests or royalty – and are flanked by fine ashlar masonry. By contrast some of the steps are just carved out of the rock. At the top you come to a platform with the columns and piers of two anterooms, beyond which is a large light well – when suddenly you notice that the end wall, the back wall of the light well, is blank and there is no grand way out to match the grand way in. This paradox is a typical Minoan surprise, but as you continue the tour you will see that it makes sense. These small exits lead to important state rooms and the Central Court: the *chiaroscuro* effect of coming into the bright sunlight of the Court or of the Peristyle Hall **74** would be all the greater for having passed through these dim corridors. Visitors would have been impressed, even bewildered, as they were by the contrast of light and shade in Bernini's original plan for the Piazza of St. Peter's. To return to Phaistos, such small exits from such a magnificent entrance made it easier to check visitors or to stop rioters trying to get in.

The anterooms at the top of the Grand Staircase are small and narrow: **68**, the first, is paved with gypsum and was separated from **69** by doors – the indents in the piers were for the doorposts. The columns and piers are surprisingly large, so that these tiny rooms would have been in deep shade while the sun shone down on the staircase and on the light well **69a**. Off **69** is a small guardroom **70** now shown by a concrete platform – as there is at the West Entrance to Knossos – and opposite it on the North side is the entrance of a passage which immediately turns back to the West and goes up three steps so that you have no idea where it is going. In fact it leads to the Peristyle Hall **74**. Otherwise, you can continue straight ahead from **69** into the large area of the light well and towards its blank back wall, leaving by a small door in the South-East corner. From the landing the other side of the door you can either go up to the left to the Peristyle Hall or down to the right to the area of the storerooms and the Central Court. A drain in the South-West corner of the light well collected rain water.

The Peristyle Hall **74** should not be missed. If you have taken the stairs up to the North from the South-East corner of the light well, you come to a gypsum-paved anteroom **75**, beyond which is the Peristyle Hall, one of the most important rooms in the palace. It is like a cloister, or a Roman *atrium,* being open in the middle. There may originally have been a garden, but now the remains of a prepalatial house are exposed. The Hall was open to the North, to the view of Psiloriti, with a verandah **93** paved with lozenge-shaped gypsum slabs outlined with red plaster in the interstices. These two rooms were closely connected to the royal living rooms below by staircases **51** and **76**.

To the North-West are traces of buildings whose purpose I do not know. You can come back into **71** and **69** by a circuitous passage which was designed so as not to interrupt the unity and privacy of the Peristyle Hall. Note in **72** a column base, whose exact purpose is still unknown. The recess in the outside wall suggests that there was a window on the floor above.

At the bottom of the stairs from the South-East corner of the light well **69** you can either turn left on to the Central Court – though this entrance was blocked up during the later life of the New Palace – or go straight on into **25**, or turn right down a passage. At the end of this short passage, before you turn left again into **38**, you can see the Old Palace storerooms through a gate. They were covered when the New Palace was built. The pithoi have been left in position – the pattern on the second pithos on the right is typical of Middle Minoan II at Phaistos. (Some of this type were exported to Knossos.) Turn back now to **38**, which has a gypsum floor, about half a metre below the level of **25**, and belongs with the storerooms to the Old Palace. Beyond **38**, and below the guardroom **70**, are the remains probably of a bath, behind a restored blocking wall.

Room **25** is large and was paved with gypsum. It is divided down the middle, where it fronts onto the continuation of passage **26**, by column bases: the third base, by the Central Court, is oval. This is unusual and the architect may have intended that it should both remain in symmetry with the other columns and yet carry a load as heavy as that which the pillars along the rest of the West side of the Central Court were carrying.

A bronze pivot was found by the South pillar in room **25** and a hole for another by the North. The doors they held would have closed against the central oval column and would have been large, a total width of 4.85 m. It is not common to close doors against a column rather than a pier, and the excavators thought that because of this, and because of the blocking of the passage, the area was sometimes rearranged. Room **25** was obviously much used in the life of the palace since it has such a central position, but we can only guess at what its use was. Most likely it was an office for the storerooms down the passage.

The storerooms are similar to those at Knossos except that they do not have cists, or boxes, set in the floor. Several querns, mortars and presses were found in them and can be seen; in **33**, at the far end on the North side (on the right) is equipment for keeping olive oil, three pithoi, a basin to catch the drips, a clay stool to stand on to look inside the pithoi, and a raised platform in the centre so that one would not get one's feet wet or slip in the grease. The floor slopes down to the North where a hole collected the spillage. The walls were lined with gypsum, which still shows signs of the fire that destroyed the New Palace of Phaistos in about 1450. In **37** (the first storeroom to the North) mud plaster is still on the walls. Look for the cavities left by the straw used to temper the plaster. **30** the other side of the passage has gypsum slabs at the South end, which are in fact part of the floor of room **VII** of the Old Palace reused. The walls between **30** and **31** and between **36** and **37** you will see are especially thick, and the pillar in the passage is aligned on them. This should be recognisable by now as the clue to a room on the floor above, occupying the space over rooms **27** to **30** and **33** to **36** and part of the passage. The recesses on the outside walls show it would have had two windows on the West side overlooking the West Court and small ones on the North over the Grand Staircase and on the South. This restored room over the storerooms can be compared to those over the storerooms at Knossos but unlike them, it was exposed on three sides. Another thicker wall between **25** and **32** gives another indication of a wall on the floor above.

Little is preserved of the South-West part of the New Palace, and what is, is difficult to understand. Several rooms seem to have been used for religion, as were those around the Temple Repositories in the South-West part of Knossos. Rooms **8–11** form one unit: **8** and **10** could be reached directly from outside the palace – in the Old Palace the shrine at the foot of the Grand Staircase was similarly accessible – and **9** and **11** are interior rooms. Passage **12** leads to other rooms, which include two baths, **19**, with a very burnt gypsum column base, and a tall stone lamp lying in the bath, and **21**. In the passage **12** notice a plastered recess, where figurines or offerings may have been put. You can look down from the edge of the hill here onto the South-West rooms of the Old Palace, preserved to two and three stories. Here is conclusive proof that the Minoans could construct highrise buildings at a fairly early stage in their history.

The Central Court measures about 51.50 m. × 22.30 m., or 170 × 80 Minoan feet and is paved with limestone flags (Plate 27). It is aligned North to South. On either side of the long axis is a portico or verandah, which provided shade from the sun at midday and would have been a pleasant place to sit in the mornings and evenings. On the West side you will see that the paving does not extend to the West edge and that there are column bases at a lower level, now

27   The North end of the flagged Central Court of Phaistos is surprisingly frontal for
Minoan architecture: the entrance to passage **41** is flanked by half-columns (seen later
at the Treasury of Atreus at Mycenae) and niches for sentries.

shown in pits: these bases probably belong to the Old Palace, or possibly the first
phase of the New Palace, and would have been part of a verandah similar to that
on the East side of the Court. In the North-West corner of the Central Court is
what appears to be a mounting block. On one of its stones is a double axe sign. It
has been suggested that, if bull games were held in the Central Courts of the
palaces, this was where people jumped off to somersault on the bull's horns, but
it may be that this block is just a stand for tubs of flowers, or possibly an altar.
The pithoi beside it were placed there by the excavators and belong to the Late
Minoan IIIB period of re-inhabitation of Phaistos. Similar pithoi can be seen in
the Propylaea **21** of Knossos.

    The formal North end of the Central Court (Plate 27) is unique in Minoan
architecture: a central doorway, flanked by half-columns, recesses and walls. (It
is a pleasant thought that this was excavated by Italians.) The recesses were
surely for sentries to guard the door to passage **41**, which is the way to the North
Court and the royal apartments from the Central Court. They were decorated
with frescoes with a simple lozenge pattern. The half-columns which frame the
door, originally of wood on stone column bases, are especially interesting as
they are the forebears of the stone half-columns which framed the doors of
Mycenaean tholos tombs. The carved half-columns of the Treasury of Atreus at
Mycenae can be seen reconstructed in the National Museum in Athens and in
the British Museum, and on Westport House in Ireland. It is quite possible that
the wooden half-columns of Phaistos were similarly carved.

    The door of passage **41** was made to be shut. The pivot holes either side show
that it was a double door, possibly of folding shutters which could have been
secured by bolts in the smaller holes along the threshold. Inside the door is
another recess for a sentry, decorated with a lozenge fresco like those outside.
The man stationed here guarded access to and from the Peristyle Hall **74** and
other rooms on that level which could be reached by staircase **42** and its return,

99

which would have been over **43**. (There is a pithos under the stairs on the ground floor, at the end of **43**.) On the upper level there would have been a large room over rooms **44-46** and another over rooms **58-61** and **91-92** to the East (the right) of passage **41**. Graham has argued that this may well have been a dining hall, in a similar position to those inferred at Mallia and Zakro.

Passage **41** has a central drain and so may have been open to take rainwater off the rooms either side, which may have had overhanging eaves or projecting waterspouts. This passage leads to the South-West corner of the North Court **48** rather than to its middle, which again introduces complexity into the design of the palace.

The North Court **48** is an enclosed space flanked by ashlar masonry. It links the rooms either side of passage **41** with the royal apartments on the North edge of the palace, and both with the East entrance. A puzzling feature is the double wall enclosing passage **47** at the West end of the Court. Perhaps what you see was used only for storage, while above there could have been a passage connecting the room restored over **44-46** with staircase **51** and so with the royal apartments.

Off the North Court to the East is an area **49** which is almost as large and has equally fine ashlar masonry, which should indicate that it was open to the sky (gypsum, which is more perishable, being used for surfaces under cover). Its walls are impressive, although the area now seems like a tank. We do not know what it was used for. Graham suggests that it may have been a pen for animals awaiting slaughter for the royal household; but it seems too good to use for animals, and the noise and smell could have been offensive to royalty if their private rooms were nearby. I think instead that **49** was a walled garden.

On the North side of the North Court you see through a hole in the ancient wall, and through the passage and probable service room below staircase **51**, into room **50**, now partly roofed with concrete. This room is one of the royal apartments of Phaistos, all of which have been closed to the public to prevent damage. As restored, it is a pleasant room with gypsum slabs and red plaster, gypsum dado and bench, and four columns. Behind it to the West are the passage and stairs **51** which lead to the Peristyle Hall **74**, which you could also reach from the North exit of room **50** by the passage and stairs **76**. Another important room **77-79** can be reached by passage **76**: it is roofed with plastic and opens onto a verandah **85** on the North edge of the hill. Its outlook onto the mountains is obscured by trees planted by the excavators.

Room **77-79** is divided into three parts, as is the Hall of the Double Axes at Knossos with its light well, and it was probably used for functions similar to those of the Hall of the Double Axes. If you enter from **76**, you can go straight through the middle part **77** to reach the verandah. At the East end a light well **78** is separated by two columns: it has a rain collector in its North-East corner. The more important part of the room is the West end **79**, which is divided from the middle part and from the verandah by piers and doors – again you are reminded of the Hall of the Double Axes at Knossos. At the South-West corner of the room a door opens onto a dogleg passage **80**, which goes up a slight ramp to the bath **83** and its anteroom **81**. White wall plaster is still in position in this passage.

The bath and the rooms around it have been cut into the side of the hill, perhaps so as not to interrupt the view of the Peristyle Hall and its loggia above. The bath was lined with gypsum, which makes it very unlikely that it was actually filled with water, as water can in time dissolve gypsum. West of the bath are two small rooms: the inner one may have been used as a dressing room, and the outer one, with a hollowed stone connected to a drain, was a lavatory. These details are like those of the Queen's Rooms at Knossos; but the general arrangement of this large private suite on the North edge of the palace, complete with bath and its private view, has its parallel at Mallia. There, however, royalty probably looked out onto a garden, not onto Psiloriti.

If you walk along the edge of the hill to the East, you come to some buildings of the Old Palace or more likely of the first phase of the New Palace. The first has a row of mudbrick boxes, two of which are faced with white plaster. The Phaistos Disc, a clay disc impressed either side with picture-signs set in a spiral, was found in one of the boxes. Neither its use nor its ultimate provenance have been determined, nor its language, if any. It may be an import, even from outside Crete. An attractive suggestion has been that it is a primitive astronomical or astrological chart, its signs representing the stars.

Further along to the East is another building of interest of the same date **103**, a large room which was probably a peristyle: if so, it anticipates the placing of the royal rooms of the New Palace on the North side, and also the plan of Peristyle Hall **74**. Room **103** has four large pillars with columns between and was probably open in the centre. A drain led rainwater to the edge of the hill. In the North wall is a door, and there were probably windows to bring in light and the view. To the South a long flight of steps goes up to the East Court and the East entrance.

The East entrance is a double one, like the North entrance at Mallia, and has a slight shift of axis from one doorway to the other. Each door was single and large, as you can see from the large rectangular cuttings for the doorposts on the South side of each threshold. On three sides of the porch are stone benches.

Passage **52** leads from the porch down a ramp to the North Court, while off it to the South is the East Court and further along to the South another sloping passage **56** by which you can reach the passage **62** that connects the Central and the East Courts. On the West side of passage **56** is the walled area **49**, which I have suggested was a garden. The East side of the passage also has a well built facade – notice the masons' marks – at the back of which are some small rooms thought to have been used by craftsmen. In the East Court beyond is a semi-circular construction behind wire which, to judge from the pieces of copper or bronze waste still adhering, was a foundry. Passage **62** leads off from the South-West corner of the East Court to the Central Court. In that corner are traces of an oval building, later used as a cistern.

From the East Court walk to the trees on the East edge of the hill, and there turn back to face the palace. In front of you is perhaps the most attractive part of Phaistos where the Minoans' skill in using the natural surroundings can be seen at its very best. The East Wing before you is a self-contained suite, with its own peristyle court abutting onto the rocks – and a view down the plain to the Lasithi mountains – its own hall which could be divided internally, its own bath, and a bench outside the door to the Central Court where people might

28 Peristyle Hall **64** in the East Wing of Phaistos, a small cloister in a self-contained part of the palace. The column bases stand on the rock.

have waited before they were admitted, or a porter sat protecting the privacy of those inside.

The column bases of this peristyle hall **64** were placed on the rock, and are still preserved in the North-West corner (Plate 28). A floor of plaster was laid down, and an open drain cut. The rock rises on the South, and at the South-East corner three broad steps go down to traces of paving outside. North of the steps the palace wall continues still, but South of it the rock seems to have been used as the facade.

At the North-West corner of the peristyle double doors open onto the main room **63**, which was divided into the room proper and its anteroom by another set of double doors. Remains of a wall and passage on the West side of the main room probably indicate a staircase to the floor above. The anteroom has two

29   The rock cut back to accommodate a wall in the East Wing of Phaistos.

exits, a short dogleg passage down steps to the Central Court, and a door to the bath and other rooms. The East wall here was built against the rock which was cut back, an interesting contrast (Plate 29). Beyond, a room with column bases set on a lower level probably dates from the Old Palace.

Outside the entrance to the East Wing from the Central Court is a bench and, next to it, what was perhaps a plastered stone tank. There are remains of other things like it to the North. Their purpose is unknown, but, as they are plastered, they were probably intended for holding liquids. I wonder if we have here a Minoan aquarium. As for the East Wing, we do not know who lived in it. Perhaps it was the son of the ruler of Phaistos who, as a boy, played with the fish in the tanks beside the Central Court.

7 Ayia Triadha

Ayia Triadha is the most pleasing of the Minoan palaces. It is particularly attractive, like Phaistos, in the early spring when the mountains are still under snow while the sun shines in the plain and flowers bloom in the rooms of the palace. Then it is a delight to walk to Ayia Triadha from Phaistos. It takes about half an hour. The path runs at the bottom of the Phaistos ridge along the North side. You pass orange and apricot groves, and at the other end of the ridge is Ayia Triadha. Having gone past its two Early Minoan tholos tombs – behind the smaller one is the tomb where the Ayia Triadha sarcophogus (p. 45) was found – you arrive at the Minoan town. The palace at the other end of the town, if approached this way, is much more of a surprise than if you have taken the car road from Phaistos when you see the whole building spread before you the moment you arrive. If you have to drive to Ayia Triadha, you can still arrive at the town end if you return to the main road (from Heraklion) and continue towards the sea for about 3 km. to a small and almost illegible sign on the left pointing to a dirt road to Ayia Triadha in the olive trees. Drive down this road and park at the end by the river, the Yeropotamos, which waters the plain of the Mesara. Cross the river (on stepping stones, or wading, or on a donkey which may appear with a driver) and follow the path through orchards which are as rich as the Garden of Eden and in five minutes you will reach the tholos tombs and Ayia Triadha.

Ayia Triadha is a difficult site to understand. This is partly because there are two main periods of its occupation, a Late Minoan I (New Palace) phase and a re-inhabitation with rebuilding in Late Minoan III, and it is not always easy to distinguish which is which. Another difficulty is that Ayia Triadha has never been properly published: the only accounts of its excavation are skimpy preliminary reports of the early years of this century. This has meant that there has been less informed discussion of the buildings and what has been found in them, and that Ayia Triadha is not as well known as it ought to be.

As you will see, it is placed just above the plain looking out towards the sea to the West over olive trees (and Tymbaki air strip). In Minoan times the sea probably came right up to the foot of the palace ridge. If this is so, the plain with olive trees is only the recently formed delta of the Yeropotamos river. The small – one hesitates to call it a Central Court as the palace buildings do not run round each side – the small Court is unusual in that it is placed East-West, unlike those of the other palaces, while in the town the row of shops is aligned North-South on Psiloriti which is the alignment of the Central Court of Phaistos.

The row of shops (Plate 30) is the pincipal building in the town. It faces West on to the sea, and opposite it, across a small *agora* or market place, are the dwelling houses of the town. A large number are exposed, though many of them are preserved only as basements: there are some well made walls of ashlar, some with small packing stones between the courses, and a quite large house

N.B. There is no generally agreed system of numbering
the rooms of Ayia Triadha.

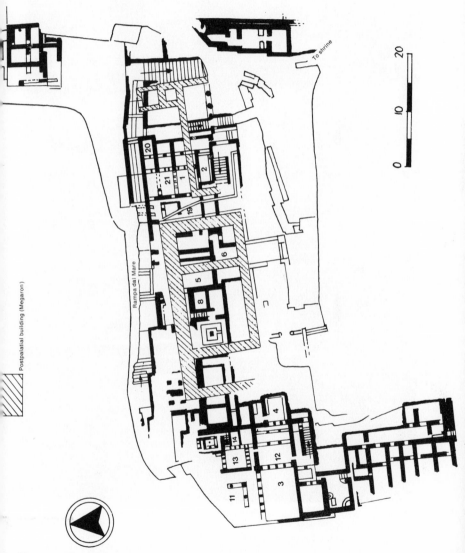

Fig. 10.   Plan of the Palace of Ayia Triadha.

30   The row of shops behind a portico in the town of Ayia Triadha faces on to a
small *agora* or market place: an early example of a *stoa*, such as that reconstructed in
the Agora of Athens. If you have come by foot along the valley, you will have
arrived at the far end of the row. A little beyond are the two tholos tombs of Ayia
Triadha.

stands out in the centre of the town. The date of the row of shops is uncertain: perhaps Late Minoan I, or perhaps Late Minoan III, as the Italian excavators would like.

The shops in the row are all regular in size, and all have large threshold blocks. Their portico had a roof supported by the row of pillars, some of which have a second block still standing – on others you can see the dowel holes to hold a wooden sleeper, above which there may have been another block or a lighter superstructure, possibly of mud bricks. Between the pillars are small column bases which shortened the span and could have been part of a system of letting down awnings to keep out the afternoon sun. At the far end of the row, if you have come to Ayia Triadha the way I have suggested, steps lead up to another house, on a different alignment, while the path winds around the outside and brings you to a Minoan verandah below the terraces of the custodian's house. Another flight of steps takes you to yet more houses which are set above the palace. Beyond them in the South-East corner of the excavated area is a shrine, which could be divided by doors into an anteroom and the shrine proper. Its floors and walls were decorated with a Late Minoan I marine fresco which is on display in the Heraklion Museum – in Late Minoan III it was again in use, and clay tubular offering stands of that period were found on the floor in front of the bench at the end of the Shrine. There may perhaps have been a wooden statue of a deity on the bench.

Below the shrine is the Court around which the palace is built in an L-shape (Fig. 10): almost all you see now is below the level of the Court – as on the East side at Knossos – but there is plenty of evidence to show that there was an upper floor. Many objects were found fallen down, the Harvester Vase among them. The Court is small since there is little space on this small ridge. At the East end you will recognise pyramidal double axe stands marking the sanctity and importance of this place, as outside the Storerooms at Knossos (Plate 15). On the North side some of the pavement is still preserved. To the West along the saddle is a portico, with rectangular flagstones and a column base, which belongs with the walls to the North that are quite clearly built over the palace. These walls seem to form a rectangular hall, possible a *megaron* of mainland Greek Mycenaean type (that is, a rectangular hall with its only entrance through a porch on one side, and often having a central hearth), that must be later than the palace. The pottery of this later building is Late Minoan III but, until Ayia Triadha is better published, we do not know when this resettlement began.

We shall go down into the palace by the staircase to the East of the ramp over the two prominent drains. These stairs are of gypsum and bring you to rooms which are interesting for their details – benches, drains, windows and stairs – and for the general excellence of their finish, which is one of the characteristics of Ayia Triadha. At the foot of these stairs is a room with benches, beyond which a window opens onto a light well (Plate 31). To the South of this light well the large blocks are probably the foundations of the Court, and there is a surprisingly well built drain. You can squeeze in to have a look. On the East side a window reveals a staircase which is the continuation of a passage running North (your left) to join a ramp inside the outer wall of the palace.

At the bottom of the staircase you have come down from the Court, turn left

31 Ashlar light well and window for room **2** at Ayia Triadha, with a gypsum bench in room **1** to the right. Similar windows opening on to light wells can be seen at Tylissos House A (Plate 44) and at Knossos (Plate 21).

into a room **2** which is lit from a window opening into a light well. The next room **1** was also lit from this light well, and room **21** beyond, reached through multiple doors, was lit by yet another light well. The rooms are faced with gypsum, the light wells with ashlar. Between the multiple doors in room **21** and its light well is a small porch, whose roof was held up by a column resting on a base of serpentine (the stone most used by the Minoans for vases). Beyond **21** another room **20** is lit by a North window, outside which is a stepped ramp open to the sky.

How these rooms connect with the storerooms is difficult to decide, since the two prominent drains have destroyed so much around. The drain to the West (nearer the sea) is of Late Minoan III date and belongs with the *megaron*. The drain to the East, as restored, makes nonsense descending through the air from the Court, a coarse stone drain in the middle of fine gypsum. Either the drain was originally much lower (and so has been wrongly restored) or there was an earthquake followed by rebuilding during the life of the palace, when this part of the palace could have been abandoned and the great drain installed. To the North of the drains is an entrance passage to the palace, and beyond is the so-called *Rampa dal Mare* which separates the palace from the town. The excavators thought that the sea came up to Ayia Triadha in Minoan times.

Storerooms **6, 18, 5** and **8** are on two levels, the level where you are standing and a mezzanine level above. On the lower level are pithoi (some wired off), and up the storeroom stairs you can look into a room with five stands of gypsum for pithoi. The stands are very badly burnt, from the destruction by fire of Ayia Triadha around 1450, as is natural if oil and other combustibles were stored here. At the top of this small staircase is a small room to the right with a central pillar and burnt gypsum flagstones.

Return to the North facade and continue on round to the elegant public rooms at the North-West corner, which are difficult to reconstruct in the imagination as so much has fallen away. However, the quality of building of the rooms and their courts, and the views to Psiloriti and the plain and the sea, make this one of the most delightful sets of rooms in Minoan architecture.

You come to a small anteroom which has three column bases and the hole for the fourth – I am not sure if this room was open in the centre or the columns helped to support the floor above. A door at the South-East corner leads into the room which had the frescoes of the woman (goddess, or priestess?) in the garden and of the cat chasing pheasants. This room was divided in two by doors. In the West half of the room a large set of Linear A tablets was found, which suggests that it may have been used as the counting house. At its North-West corner is a peristyle court; and off this court and off room 14 is a series of rooms at the back of which is the main room of the palace 4. The main room has a gypsum bench round three sides and gypsum dadoes on the walls. Holes show where beams held the rubble filling of the walls. It is a cool room, and pleasant to sit in, and to look out from. It was lit by stone standard lamps: one was found in the room, and two more either side of the entrance of the small side room. This room has a low gypsum bench on the floor, which was the base of a divan. Imagine it covered with mattresses and rugs and cushions, as a similar divan in the Dressing Room by the Queen's Room at Knossos would have been.

The main room was shut by double doors. Beyond the doors are two rows of column bases, with a drain below the first row, which suggests that one of the long narrow spaces was open to the sky, probably that between the rows of columns. Beyond is another room, which opens into a large hall at the edge of the excavations. This hall had views of the sea and opened through double doors into the peristyle court, which I should imagine was itself open for a better view of Psiloriti.

South of the main room are a stairway and its return (with a cupboard below the stairs) and a small light well with a dowelled column base – notice the contrast between the ashlar masonry exposed to the weather and the faced rubble walls of the main room. Off this light well double doors take you into a room to the West containing pithoi, and there are two separate exits to the South. One exit goes into a flagged room with gypsum dadoes and three large plaster vats, perhaps the workroom of the fresco painters (the vats are like those in the 'School Room' 42 at Knossos), and the other goes into a pillar basement which probably supported a room above.

Beyond these rooms on the South is a series of storerooms with windows at the back which open onto a passage which is dug into the hillside. These storerooms have large threshold blocks, as the shops in the colonnade in the town do, and may have been craftsmen's workshops. Their regular arrangement is like that of the row of shops, and perhaps they were the predecessors of that row, if that is of Late Minoan III date. From one of these rooms came the carved serpentine Chieftain Cup (p. 45). This area is bordered by a paved room running North-South which would have joined the road on the North side of the Palace.

You can scramble back up to the Court and have a look at the Venetian church of St. George and its frescoes.

8 Mallia

About six hours' walk from Heraklion, or half to three-quarters of an hour in a car, you reach the small, fertile plain of Mallia. It is watered from wells, and is hot in summer and exposed to the North wind. Towards the East end of the plain beyond the modern village is the Minoan palace, on a route to East Crete through the gorge of Selinari and over the pass of Vrakhasi. It is set on a low hillock at the end of a spur of the North side of the Lasithi mountains. These mountains dominate the plain of Mallia. You are always aware that they are there, even though the ground around the palace is flat and exposed. To the North it is a few minutes' walk to the sea from the palace, past the cemetery of Khrysolakkos where the famous gold pendant of insects eating a fruit was part of the offerings for the dead; and the so-called 'Aegina Treasure' quite probably came from this cemetery also (Plate 5).

The placing of the palace of Mallia on such low ground so close to the sea has long been thought conclusive proof that the peace the Minoans enjoyed was secured by a navy. This idea may be still correct, but a wall has been found in recent years which may be a defence wall of the town. It is 1.75 m. thick, too thick to be the wall of a normal building, and dates from Middle Minoan III: it is to the South of House Z β to the East of the palace. If it is a defence wall, and not say just a grandiose boundary wall, it is unique at the moment in Minoan Crete; but outside Crete there are indisputable defence walls of this time at places such as Ayia Irini on Kea, where there was a strong Minoan influence. It may well be that there really was some danger from invaders or pirates.

The palace is a relatively simple building, and it seems the one most in keeping with the country around. The walls are made of the hard grey limestone and softer red sandstone that you see scattered in the fields, and the mudbricks were burnt red in the fire that destroyed the palace about 1450. As red is the colour of the local earth, they may have been red even before the fire. Mallia is not grand or pretentious – there is no gypsum used, for instance – nor is it dramatic, but its quiet character and its sense of fitting its surroundings are refreshing after the other palaces. Mallia grows on the visitor, and with every visit reveals more of its especial beauty, both in its setting and in itself.

The plan of the palace (Fig. 11) is as easy to follow as that of Phaistos. There are few buildings on its South and East sides, but the North and West sides are built up and front onto an internal North Court as well as onto the West and Central Courts as you would expect. A corridor with storerooms backs on to the West facade, and between that and the Central Court are grander rooms with a hall, a pillar shrine and steps and staircases – a smaller version of the layout of the West side of Knossos. On the North and East sides a portico runs round the Central Court, with, behind it on the North, a pillar room which supported a large hall above. A passage leads out beside this room to the North Court (now partly obscured by a later building on a different alignment) and past storerooms to the North entrance, where a street takes you into the town. The royal private apartments are at the North-West corner of the Palace. On the east side of the Central Court behind the portico are storerooms for oil, which are now locked up and cannot be visited (some vases were stolen from them). On the South side are workrooms, and an elegant wide paved entrance which must have been the main entrance to the palace.

The French excavators have divided the palace into areas (*quartiers*) marked by Roman numerals, in which separate rooms are marked by Arabic numerals. Thus **IX 2** refers to the large room at the North end of the Central Court (probably a kitchen) and **XVI 1** to the area of the *kernos*, a term which will be explained below. I shall follow their system.

You arrive at Mallia outside the West Court, which has crazy paving as do the West Courts of Knossos and Phaistos. A raised walk of flagstones crosses it from North to South, but on a different alignment from the West facade, and so perhaps parallel to a line of the facade of the Old Palace. Notice also a regular line in the paving closer to the Palace wall and parallel to it in the South part of the Court. We do not know what it distinguishes: it may be just an instance of the Minoan love of making patterns when they paved areas or it may also be related to the line of the Old Palace buildings. The main raised walk goes South toward the eight circular pits or *koulouras* at the South-West corner of the Palace which, unlike those at Knossos and Phaistos, are arranged in two rows. Four of them still have central pillars to support a roof (Plate 32). I think it is

32   The eight *koulouras* of Mallia, though not as deep as those of Knossos, are an impressive sight. Their central pillars would have supported the roof; and it is almost certain that they were silos for corn.

almost certain that they were silos to hold corn (as were the *koulouras* of the other palaces) but, as one at least was plastered, the French excavators thought that they were cisterns for water: *'on aurait eu de la sorte un véritable château d'eau destiné à l'approvisionment du palais'*. They suggested that the koulouras were used to collect rainwater from the gutters, but a difficulty with this theory is that no channels are preserved leading into them, as have been found at Tylissos where there is an undoubted cistern. The writers of the recent French guide to Mallia are convinced that they are for corn, however.

From the *koulouras* you can continue along the South facade to reach the South Entrance, but we shall return North through the West Court. The West facade has been dilapidated by ploughing, and has been restored in the plan (Fig. 11). However it is like Knossos in having large projections and bays which vary the outline but in fact are no more than the skins of the rooms on the inside. There are also at least three recesses, each in the centre of its bay or projection, which should mark the windows of the missing floor above. At the North end notice the remains of an outside shrine: two column bases to hold the roof and an altar base behind. The wall that continues the line of these bases, the West wall of **III 3**, has been doubled by an extra course of stones, each stone of which has a socket or post hole in it. These stones continue round on the South side into the bay, but I am not sure for what they were used. They may have supported an awning which is not connected with the shrine at all, but with the West entrance of the palace. People could have sat under it while waiting to go in or an attendant could have vetted petitioners here.

The West entrance is almost hidden and could even have been an after-thought in the construction of the New Palace. It brings you along a passage into the Long Corridor, where you can see at once the different materials used in building this palace: large sandstone blocks; small, rough, grey pieces of lime-stone; large, red mud bricks; and red mud plaster, sometimes faced with white lime plaster. Halfway along, to the South, the Corridor has been blocked off by a wall (Plate 33) which separates group **I** of the storerooms from group **VIII**. Notice the massive sandstone thresholds to the entrance passage and to **I 5** and **I 6**. The piers in **I 4** and **I 5**, which supported columns in the hall above, flank the window recess in the outside wall. The hall we are restoring would then have occupied the whole of area **I** on the floor above; while **I 1** below it seems to have been a strongroom since it could be reached only from the upper floor. If we look now at the plan for the thicker walls and remember where the window recesses are on the outside wall, we can restore other upper rooms, one over **VIII** and another over **III**. There were doubtless more, but it is difficult to establish what happened on the upper floor in the North-West corner of the palace since so little is preserved on the ground anyway: these larger rooms we have imagined over the storerooms remind us again of those we have recon-structed at Knossos and Phaistos and reinforce our suggestions for restoring those two palaces.

Storerooms **VIII** are relatively isolated and thus more secure. You can reach them from the other parts of the palace only through **VII** and **II**, areas devoted to religion and royalty which would have been difficult to penetrate. At Knossos one group of storerooms is similarly more difficult of access.

33 The blocking wall across the Long Corridor at Mallia separates group **I** and
group **VIII** of the storerooms. It is made of mud bricks, held by layers of mud, and is
faced with white lime plaster.

If you continue straight across the Corridor from the West entrance, you come into three small storerooms **II 1** where twenty-seven vases were found *in situ*. Twenty-three of them were in the first room of **II 1** including one on the projection of each of the steps on the North side. In the doorway into this room from the Corridor, notice where the doorposts stood.

Area **VI** where you now come is not easy to understand as the visible remains belong to both the Old and the New palaces. You enter **VI 2**, a large and secluded room, whose only other entrance is a narrow door from the so-called Loggia **VI 1**. The floor of **VI 2** is at a lower level, and belonged to the Old Palace. On it were found a ceremonial axe carved as a leopard and the famous long ceremonial sword with an acrobat in relief on its pommel. These were doubtless sacred offerings, and the room itself a religious treasury. In the North-East corner is a fine stone-chip floor, and on the other side there may have been a window opening onto **IV 9** and **10** which, with built-in benches like those in a recently discovered shrine at Mycenae, may have been an inner sanctuary. (In the excavation report these two rooms are thought to be the workshop of an ivory carver.) North of **VI 2** is **VI 5**, another blind room with no obvious opening – it is paved with flagstones and, being at a higher level, may belong to the New Palace. One must have reached it from above, but its use is unclear. The excavators have suggested it was a bathroom, on the strength of a channel on the North which runs into the lower **IV 7**. To the East are two small stores **VI 3** and **VI 4**.

A small staircase takes you from **VI 2** into the Loggia **VI 1**. The Loggia faces onto the Central Court, and is approached by a flight of steps in the middle of which is a pillar base to support the roof or the flight above. (This same technique is used on the large staircase beside the so-called Throne Room at Knossos.) On the line of these steps at the back of the Loggia two stones are set in the crazy paving of the floor, which the excavators think may have been bases for altars or for tables for pouring libations out. This may be right since the Loggia is undoubtedly a large and important room. The reason it is raised may have been so that people could watch rituals being performed in it from the Court outside. Furthermore it has the same position in the palace as the Throne Room does at Knossos, which as we have seen (p. 63) was more likely a cult room, and both have ancillary rooms behind. It is most probable then that this part of the palace was the religious centre of Mallia.

Two steps lead down from the Loggia onto a landing in the Grand Staircase and continue across it and down into the Hall **VII 3** (Plate 34), and some other steps come off the Grand Staircase at a higher level down into the Hall. This double access links the Loggia and the Hall more closely. As for the Grand Staircase, it's existence is conclusive proof, if any more is needed, of the important missing floor above. The Staircase was probably open to the sky, since it has gutters.

The Hall is placed in the middle of the West side of the Central Court, the position that the Hall at Zakro has. Its main part **VII 3** measures 9 × 8.30 m., but its total length along the Court is much greater even though it was probably divided by doors into several rooms. Since the wall of the Court is so thin, I think it could have been two stories high, but was not strong enough to hold an

34   Landing on the Grand Staircase at Mallia. The pattern of the Grand Staircase
VI 8 is interrupted by this landing, with steps coming down from the Loggia **VI 1**
and continuing across the landing down to the Hall **VII 1, 3.**

upper floor. The room then would have been a true Great Hall, like a mediaeval hall. Along the centre of the Hall is a row of column bases: the one near the entrance from the Central Court has been partly stepped and has a hole in it which could have held a door to shut off **VII 11**. The West exit from the Hall is into the Pillar Crypt **VII 4**. The two rooms are now separated by a wall, but in the Old Palace there were two columns in its place, which would have made an even larger room. Their bases can be seen below the present floor level to the North and below the wall to the South, each in line with a pillar of the Crypt.

The Pillar Crypt would have been a dark room, as are the pillar crypts that are in much the same position on the West side of Knossos (Plate 17). The ceremonies in it probably involved light. Double axe signs are carved on the pillars and, to emphasise the Crypt's religious importance, the pit and the altar base in the middle of the Central Court have been related to it, being aligned between its two pillars. Another pillar is at the West end of **VII 11**. The rest of Area **VII** was probably devoted to service rooms and storerooms, through which one can easily reach the South half of the Long Corridor with its Storerooms **VIII** and Areas **XIX** and **XX**.

Before we leave Area **VII**, notice how it stands out for the grandeur of its rooms and the quality of their building, mainly stone, whereas the adjacent storerooms are mostly made of mud brick.

The Central Court is slightly smaller than those of Knossos and Phaistos, measuring about 48 × 22 m. Some parts of it are still paved, but it is not certain if all of it was. The paved quarter circle in the North-East corner looks as if it has not just been left by the chance of time but was intended to give easy unmuddied access from the East Portico to the North Portico. If this is so, the rest of the Central Court could have been plain earth.

By the South-West corner where the South entrance meets the Central Court and up two steps is a circular stone, known as the *kernos* (Plate 35). There are thirty-four small hollows round its edge and a larger hollow in the centre. The kernos is made of the common blue-grey local limestone and is unique, though other cruder stones with small hollows hammered in them have been found at Mallia, Phaistos, and in fact at almost all excavated Minoan sites. The hollows in the Mallia kernos were presumably made to receive something; and the most plausible suggestion is that, being as many as thirty-four they were intended to receive a harvest offering of the first fruits. It is quite as likely however that the seeds were offered to be blessed and made fertile, and not fruits, or that people coming to the palace to pay their 'taxes' came in by the South entrance and gave a token of what they had brought with them. Equally it may be that only the ruler of Mallia, or sufficiently important visitors, made ceremonial offerings which could be watched by people standing on the terraces next to the kernos on the North. The room with a column on the South side of the kernos **XVI 2** was probably an anteroom connected with the ritual. (As for the rougher stones with hollows found at other Minoan sites, they could have been likewise for offerings, or perhaps for children's games.)

The South entrance is simple but impressive, being paved with large rectangular flagstones. Doors open off it either side. One opens West into Area **XVII** as soon as you come inside the palace. According to the present ground

35   The *kernos* in room **XVI** 1 at Mallia is made of the local limestone and has thirty-four small hollows round the rim. They may have held offerings of the first fruits, which people could have given when they entered the palace by the South entrance.

plan, **XVII** is a self contained unit as is **XVIII**, which can be reached only from the outside. This entry however, into **XVIII** 1, may be just a window, like that in **X** 1 in the East facade, and one may have reached these rooms originally from the upper floor.

The South wing, like the South wing of Zakro, probably contained workshops and more important rooms above with windows looking out onto the Central Court as the recesses in the facade show. You will notice on the South wall of the Central Court square pegholes which hold wooden beams (as on the Town Mosaic) and the marks of where the beams lay.

You now turn to the East side, where a modern building covers the storerooms of Area **XI**. Near the South-East corner of the Central Court is another entrance to the palace, outside which are the town houses of Area Zeta about 50 m. away. The South-East entrance brought one into the East Portico, marked by alternating pillars and column bases with round post holes between each pillar and base. The purpose of these posts was to make an enclosure for spectators at the bull games, Graham thinks; but I am not sure that such a functional explanation is the only possible answer. The posts could equally have been part of a decorative balustrade, like that round a monastic cloister. The Portico extends the length of blocks **XI** and **XII**.

The three storerooms of **XII** are still accessible, but those of **XI**, formerly one of the most interesting parts of Mallia, have been locked since the theft of two vases. If you are allowed in, you will see elaborate methods of storing oil: pithoi with bung holes; channels in the floor to take spillage to a collecting pit; stools to

36　The portico at the North end of the Central Court at Mallia was supported by columns, unlike that on the East side which had pillars, columns and posts.

stand on to look inside the pithoi; tubs to separate the oil when it was being made; and lamps and loom weights.

In the block to the North of these storerooms, Area **X**, is a room with three bays **X 1** and a window at the end. A mass of cooking pots was found here and the room may have been a pantry used for the probable dining room which Graham has suggested was on the upper floor at the North end of the Central Court.

The North end of the Central Court is enhanced by a portico which is continued into the West side of the palace (Plate 36), carrying on the line of the South wall of **X 1**. Behind the portico is a mudbrick wall, and a flight of stairs and its return to the East. To the West you can enter a room with a pillar **IX 1** and a large room with six pillars **IX 2** (Plate 37). At Zakro there is another large

37   Room **IX 2** with six pillars at Mallia lies immediately behind the portico of
Plate 36. The staircase beside the room on the East and the parallel in plan and
position with room **XXII** (the Kitchen) at Zakro suggest that the pillars supported a
dining hall above, and that the area below was for preparing the food.

room with six pillars behind a portico in this position in the palace: animal bones
were found in it, and cooking pots in an adjacent room. At Mallia cooking pots
were found in **X 1**. Both the inferred upper floor rooms were probably dining
rooms. The pillars in each of the rooms below could have supported columns in
the rooms above.

There are still two features to be mentioned in the Central Court before we
leave to look at the North wing. One is a cannonball, Venetian or later, outside
the Loggia; the other the pit in the centre covered by a plastic awning. It is about
0.25 m. deep, and is lined with mud bricks and has four mud brick stands set in
it. Burnt wood was found in the excavation. It was probably the stand for an
altar and was connected with the cult of the Pillar Crypt **VII 4**, as it is aligned
between the pillars of that room.

From the North-West corner of the Central Court a narrow paved passage
leads between the Dining Room block **IX** and the Keep **V**, past a small portico
with a column, to the North Court. The North Court is now partly obscured
by a later building **XXIII** which was put up on top of it at a different angle and
which uses some of the Minoan blocks. You will notice one with an engraved
branch sign. The building is later than the palace, but how much later is not
known: it may belong to the last years of the Minoan era, or to the Archaic or
Classical period of Early Iron Age Crete. It was probably a shrine.

This diagonal building projects into the North Court (Plate 38). On the East
and North sides of the Court in the time of the palace was a portico behind
which are two more groups of storerooms. You can see three column bases that

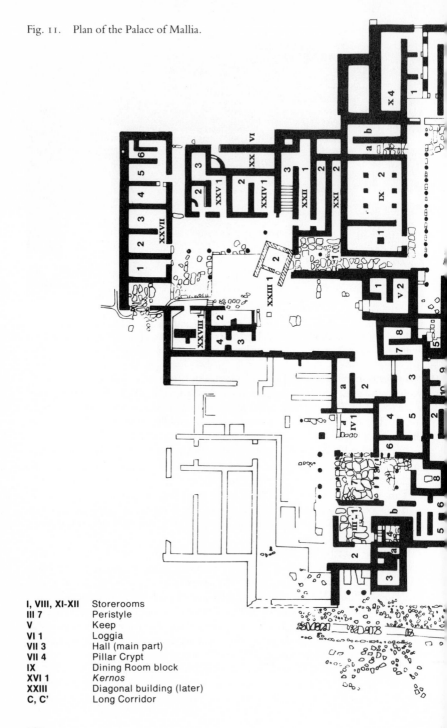

Fig. 11.   Plan of the Palace of Mallia.

I, VIII, XI-XII	Storerooms
III 7	Peristyle
V	Keep
VI 1	Loggia
VII 3	Hall (main part)
VII 4	Pillar Crypt
IX	Dining Room block
XVI 1	*Kernos*
XXIII	Diagonal building (later)
C, C'	Long Corridor

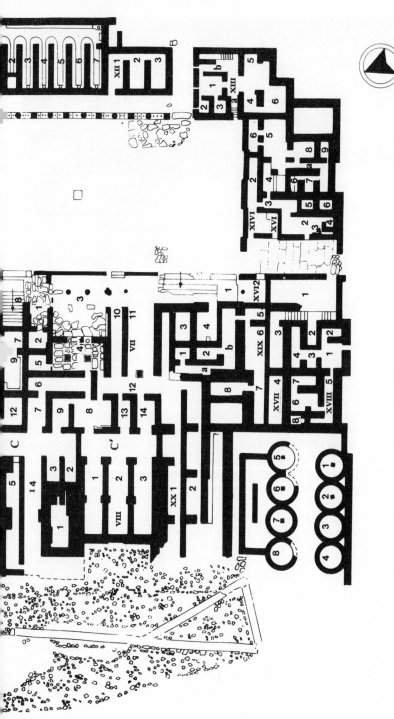

38 The later diagonal building at Mallia, set across the portico of the North Court, was probably a shrine of the end of the Minoan period or of Archaic or Classical times. It uses blocks from the palace. To the left of the pithos in the background is the North entrance of the palace; on the right are some storerooms.

define the border of the Court and the portico. Straight ahead as you enter the Court from the South is the North entrance of the palace: it is a typically complex approach, along a raised walk, through doors and then an unexpected right turn inside the porch. A drain at the North-West corner of the North Court takes the water away under the walls to the outside.

Before you leave for the North entrance, turn round at the diagonal building **XXIII** to visit the Keep Court and the royal apartments of Mallia. The Keep Court, as you see, adjoins the North Court. It is named after the Keep, the very solid building **V** in front of you, which stands out almost as the foundations of a tower. Three steps lead to the Keep, the top one being its threshold: this threshold preserves the marks of where the door swung on it, and the hole where it was secured.

Turning West (to the left) out of the Keep, you come into a small court **IV 2** with a verandah on its South side (towards the mountains). Go through the verandah, then to the right, then turn right again and then left, to come to the peristyle **III 7**, which corresponds to the Peristyle Hall **74** in much the same position at Phaistos. Adjoining its South and East sides are light wells, while to the North is a long portico which could have opened on to a garden. This possible garden would have been over the earlier grey walls now exposed. On the West side the peristyle is closed by a wall, behind which is a smaller hall: one is reminded of the Hall of the Colonnades which is back-to-back with the light well of the Hall of the Double Axes at Knossos. Indeed, the airy and spacious elegance of this part of Mallia is like that of the royal rooms on the East side of Knossos. Off this smaller hall is a bath **III 4**.

Now return to the Keep Court, through the light well **IV 1** on the East of the

39   The North entrance of Mallia seen from outside (West). Unlike the South entrance, it is small and the visitor cannot enter directly, but has to turn a corner.

peristyle, and along a corridor to reach the Keep Court, the North Court and the North entrance.

The Town

The raised walk from the North entrance of the palace brings you to the Agora (on the North, your right), a rectangular space of 29.10 × 39.80 m. – which is larger than the Central Court. It is walled on all four sides and has a plaster floor, and was built in the Old Palace period, as were the other buildings most worth visiting in the town of Mallia. (There are also several New Palace period houses you can see.) The interest of this area is that it could really have been an agora, or market place – something we could reasonably expect to find in Minoan Crete, but of which we have on the whole too little evidence. The row of shops in the town of Ayia Triadha also should be similar.

Further on to the West, under roofing, you will see a most interesting group of basements or crypts, and five storerooms for oil. The storerooms have an elaborate system for collecting spillage. The crypts are carefully built, with plastered walls and those at either end have benches. Little was found in them, which has led to the suggestion that they were used for council meetings – a possibility. They were built in the Old Palace period, destroyed and partly re-used in the time of the New Palace.

Further still to the West, under a low roof, another important group of Old Palace buildings is being excavated: Area Mu. Preliminary reports show sophisticated architecture, a Hieroglyphic accounting system and a seal maker's workshop. The use of the buildings and their relationship to the Old Palace is not yet certain.

9 Zakro

Desolate country lies on the route to Zakro. In most places the soil is poor and vegetation has been reduced to a prickly scrub which alone still survives the attention of goats. In a few spots, such as Ano Zakro (which has a Minoan country house, p. 143), springs of water give some fertility, but generally the East end of Crete is harsh and bleak. Some way below Ano Zakro the gorge of Zakro appears to the left of the road. It is one of the great sights of the island. Stop to have a look from the edge. The gorge (Plate 1) curves round to come into a tiny plain opening onto the bay of Zakro. The palace (Plate 40) is at the North end of this plain where the ground starts to rise, about 100 m. inland, and near the mouth of the gorge. When you reach it, parts may be under water, as they are for much of the year and tadpoles may be swimming in the halls of Minoan royalty. When the Minoans built the palace it was obviously set above the flood level; nowadays the fact that it is so much of the year underwater, helps to show that the East end of Crete has sunk since Minoan times. The flooding may have worsened in this century, as the course of the stream in the plain at the foot of the gorge has altered.

The importance of Zakro was in its bay which gives excellent natural protection from storms at sea. Hogarth, who excavated part of the Minoan town in the first decade of the century (and missed the palace by a few metres) watched a fleet of sponge fishermen lying up there when bound for Libya, and today caiques still use it for shelter. It is more suitable than the bay of Palaikastro to the North, being smaller and more enclosed. The Minoans appreciated this. Among the wealth of the palace were elephant tusks and copper ingots, both valuable raw materials which had probably been landed at Zakro to be taken overland to the palaces of the centre of Crete: in this way the boats could avoid having to round Cape Sidhero, the North-East tip of the island, virtually impossible for a sailing boat when the *meltemi*, which is normally a North wind, is blowing, as here it veers to the West. If Zakro was used as the nearest and safest landfall for boats bringing imports from the East, that may explain why the Minoans built such a fine, if small, palace in such a remote and poor, though exceptionally beautiful, spot. As far as we know, they did not build a palace at Palaikastro, even though it has a much larger and more fertile plain for better agriculture. As the only palace known in this part of Crete is at Zakro, it may have been intended that goods imported would come immediately under the control of royalty when they entered Crete, even if that was far away from the centre of the island.

The excavation of the palace and its surrounding town is still being carried on by Professor Platon, who will publish the results. Until that is done, only more general remarks are appropriate in a book like this, which Professor Platon has

40 General view of Zakro, before much of the town on the slope in the foreground had been excavated. The Central Court, and the Hall, in the similar position to that of Mallia, stand out. Water just visible on the far side of the palace is a reminder of the problems the Minoan builders had to cope with (the photograph was taken in August).

kindly let me make. His excavation has been one of the most exciting in Crete for its finds and, with that at Khania which was also begun in the 1960s, has made archaeologists re-think their ideas of what the Minoan civilisation was like. Both have shown that Minoan palatial culture was diffused throughout the whole island, an idea which seems obvious now but which for a long time was doubted because of lack of evidence.

The palace is small, but fine. Luckily many of its details have been preserved in the water and the mud: have a look for them as you go round. You can see evidence surviving of building techniques which have only been inferred at the other palaces, and the waterworks of Zakro are the best in Minoan Crete.

Water was the chief problem. To cope with it, drains, a cistern, a spring chamber and a well were all built or dug. The water table was probably fairly close to the surface, though below the level of the cellar-storerooms on the West side, unless they were sometimes flooded. There is no gypsum at Zakro, but white lime plaster was put between the courses of the limestone blocks. The mud bricks are well preserved: East of the kitchen a wall has tipped over, exposing its courses, and in the Shrine, the Treasury and the Archive bricks, now burnt red, were used for partition walls and for making clay boxes. Plenty of wood was used: there is evidence for it in the staircases, on thresholds, in window frames, and even at the side of the bench in **XXXIV** under the knees. Finally look at the floors, for their variety (see Fig. 13 on pp. 136–7).

You enter from the North-East along a paved street that comes from the direction of the sea. The street has a central path of white stones flanked by blue ones, though some blue stones have been used to repair gaps among the white ones. This street brings you to a portico, with a large threshold block and thick projecting ashlar walls with a rubble fill. Through the portico, where the white and blue stones continue, you come down into the North-East Court, which has been destroyed by farming as the rest of the East side has been. Two drains take storm water away from the Court to the cistern.

Walk through to the Central Court, which is smaller than those of Mallia or Phaistos, measuring about 30.30 × 12.15 m. or 100 × 40 Minoan feet as against their 170 × 80. In it are the remains of an altar. The West facade on the opposite side from that which you enter by, and built of ashlar and a lower course of grey limestone, conceals a large Hall **XXVIII**, in the same position as that at Mallia. At the North end of the West side – again like Mallia – are three openings. The central opening goes into a room **XXX** with a gravel and plaster floor, and a column base, which may have been a shrine or be somehow connected with the altar. North of it a passage **XXXI** leads to the Kitchen **XXXII** and a room **IX** with a floor of tiles surrounded by gravel and plaster. It was lit from a light well which also lights the Hall, into which the third entrance off the Central Court takes you. Smashed in pieces in the light were a bull's head rhyton and the Mountain Shrine Rhyton (see p. 45 above).

The Hall consists of an elaborate series of rooms, each slightly different from the other, like the rooms that make up the Hall of the Little Palace at Knossos. At its North end a drain takes water away from the light well, and at the South double doors lead into another room with an equally unusual floor design.

This room is of importance as it controls access between the Kitchen area on one side and the storerooms and the Shrine on the other, the places where the agricultural and industrial and artistic wealth of Zakro was kept. Notice a cupboard below stairs **X** which would have led to grander rooms over the storerooms. The storerooms are semi-basements, lit by windows onto the West Court. The West Court slopes down to the North, and was covered by terraces in the second phase of the palace's building in Late Minoan I.

The South-West corner of the palace contains a Shrine **XXIII** and Bath **XXIV**, around which are the Archive **XVI** and the Treasury **XXV**, with its workshop **XXVI** and storeroom **XXVII** – yet more evidence that art, the economy and religion were inextricably linked for the Minoans in their palaces. In the workshop flat stones are grouped in a rectangle in the South-West corner, perhaps as supports for a low wooden bench for the craftsmen, as one can see in eastern bazaars today. In **XXVII** fifteen pithoi were found. The Treasury has nine built chests of mud brick with white plaster floors. These chests contained the chalices, the rock crystal rhyton, the Egyptian stone vases adapted by the Minoans, and faience nautili and many other astonishing finds. On the floor of the Bath an elaborate marble amphora was found. **XXII** in the corner was probably another workshop, and the South-West annexe another, in the North wall of which a lavatory leads to a soakaway pit outside in the West Court.

The Shrine was a bench, now of stone, but presumably it originally had a wooden shelf on top. One is reminded of the shrine behind the Throne Room at Knossos. West of it, Linear A tablets were found by the South wall of the Archive: they had been stored on wooden shelves in three recesses in a mud-brick wall. Shelves were also used in the Pot Store **XIII** on the West side, as the excavator inferred from the way the pots had fallen.

The Kitchen **XXXII** with its six large and rough column bases which supported probably a Dining Room above is like the room under the probable dining room at Mallia: in position and arrangement the two are virtually identical. At Zakro the stairs **LII** to this Dining Room are further away than at Mallia, being separated from the Kitchen by a pantry **LI**. The stairs would have been of wood, as no stone treads were found. In the pantry were many cooking pots and by the North-East corner of the Kitchen a mass of bones was found, the debris of dinners.

You reach staircase **LI** from the Central Court through a paved verandah **XXXIV** – again as at Mallia – at the West end of which is a bench.

East of the block with the pantry and stairs is a passage **LV** and beyond it a bath **LVIII**, now with a wooden roof. On the North side of this bath is a plastered bench, and on the North and West are columns. Its position close to the main entrance of the palace may mean that it had the similar function of cleaning (or cleansing) visitors, as the bath by the North Entrance at Knossos (Plate 10) may have done.

The royal rooms on the East side of the palace have been so much destroyed that their plan rests only on the evidence of foundations. A pillared verandah on the Central Court leads into two large halls divided by multiple doors. **XXXVI** to the North was lit by a light well at its East end; **XXXVII** has a cistern or pool in the room next to it, where royalty could have bathed. The Cistern Room is floored, as are the other rooms at Zakro, with lime- and gravel-plaster which dips down to the cistern and would have drained spillages. Two column bases have been found, and a third in the North-East Court which probably came from here, which suggest that the cistern was ringed with columns to support a roof. The cistern was supplied from the spring in the Spring Chamber **LXVIII**.

By the South-East corner is the Well **XLI** with steps down to it, from which Minoan olives were recovered, their flesh still intact. On the South side were several workshops, for faience, crystal and ivory in **XLIII**, and for scent in **XLV** which is a pillar basement. A staircase and its return **XLVa**, **b**, go up to more important rooms above – as at the South end of Mallia – and the frescoes which were found here may have come from that room. Beside this block is the South entrance.

10 Gournia
and Other Towns

Gournia

Gournia is the most completely excavated Minoan town. It is set on a small hill overlooking the Bay of Mirabello, two minutes walk from the main road to Sitia and Ierapetra. It is in fact a few kilometres to the West of the Isthmus of Ierapetra, the narrowest part of Crete, and was a natural centre of communications for those travelling by land, or by sea if bad weather had not forced them to put in at Zakro. Several Near Eastern imports have been found at Gournia, which has a small cove for its harbour and a lovely view from the town of the Bay of Mirabello.

Gournia is on the North end of a ridge, like Mallia, but it is set higher above the sea than Mallia. Most of the Minoan town is built on the slopes of the ridge, to leave the ground below free for farming, but buildings could have spilt over onto the flat ground. With narrow streets winding along and up the hill, cobbled and stepped, and houses with deep basements facing onto the streets, it is very similar to a modern Cretan village. As you would expect, plenty of evidence was found that the same handicrafts were practised then as now: farming, fishing, weaving, bronzesmithery, and stone vase making. But Gournia was probably more prosperous (after due comparisons) than a Cretan village of the same size is today, as the contents of the houses show a remarkably high standard of living; for instance, the inhabitants could afford to import pottery made in Knossos. Still, it does not seem to have been as rich as Palaikastro, where substantial town houses are laid out regularly along wider streets.

The earliest occupation known at Gournia is of Early Minoan III, which was followed by a Middle Minoan phase, of which the excavators found scattered traces. Most of the town you see belongs to the period of the New Palaces and was destroyed, as were the other settlements of East Crete, in Late Minoan IB around 1450. The inhabitants, or at any rate one of them, left so suddenly that a carpenter's tool kit was found hidden in a cranny outside the door of one of the houses. Later, in Late Minoan III, parts of the town were cleared out and re-inhabited. The Shrine just to the North of Gournia's small palace is probably part of the life of this resettlement, since its contents included a clay goddess with raised arms typical of Late Minoan IIIB.

Enjoy Gournia by walking around as you please, and notice its features. The streets are about a metre and a half wide and have been laid with care, but it would be a squeeze to get past a loaded donkey. Mud bricks, mud plaster and lime plaster were all used in the building: the mud bricks found fallen intact in the palace and baked by the fire that destroyed Gournia measured 0.50 × 0.35

N.B. **20** appears twice in the original plan

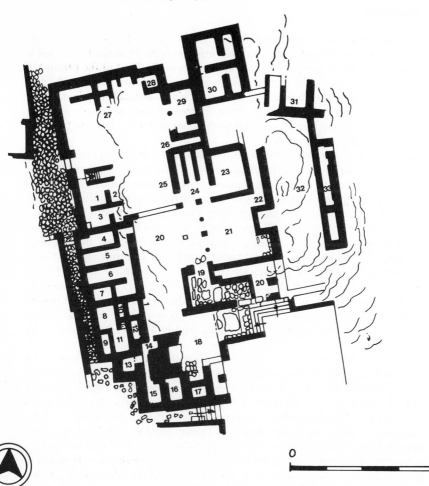

Fig. 12. Plan of the Palace of Gournia.
28 Bath

41   The small West Court outside the palace of Gournia is a miniature of those
outside the large palaces of Knossos, Phaistos and Mallia. The West facade of this
palace is indented for windows, as the others are.

× 0.085 m. There are several styles of building in stone: a large 'Cyclopean' style, one with smaller but still rounded stones, and one with longish rectangular stones wedged by small blocks. You will observe the basements and storerooms, many of which must have needed a ladder to get into as they are blind rooms now, and the stairways. Gournia is an enjoyable place to visit, particularly in the springtime; and it is a change to be somewhere so essentially domestic after marvelling at the great palaces.

There is a small palace at Gournia (Fig. 12). It is smaller than that at Zakro and could have been the house of the governor of the town or of this part of East Crete, a post he could have held by inheritance or by appointment from Knossos. The palace is at the North end of the flat top of the ridge and looks down on the town. It is the focal point of this flat top, which was probably the market place; the excavator called it the Town Court. Its situation is similar to that of the building which dominates the market place of the Archaic seventh-sixth century town of Lato near Kritsa, which can be included on a day excursion to Gournia from Heraklion and is well worth the trip.

At the South end of the Court is a smaller house which is perhaps the most interesting of those at Gournia. It has ashlar thresholds, and a large hall with a forehall, a design which may have been influenced by the Mycenaean *megara* of mainland Greece: the existence of similar *megara* has been claimed at Ayia Triadha and at Tylissos. The pottery found in this building at Gournia dates from Late Minoan III, probably the time of Mycenaean rule at Knossos, possibly from after the destruction of that palace.

'The Palace (of Gournia)', its excavator remarked, is 'not larger than an American country house of moderate size.' Like them, it was contrived to imitate in detail larger buildings, which makes it particularly valuable for the student of Minoan architecture as evidence of what the Minoans' habits and preferences were and what they thought worth copying. For instance, although the palace is on the whole made of rough masonry, the West and South facades – those you see from the West Court (Plate 41) and the Town Court – have been faced with ashlar. Even so, the ashlar does not continue all the way along the South side, though it is possible that the rough masonry which begins where the ashlar stops, may have been rendered with plaster to improve its looks. The West Court is a miniature of those of the larger palaces and lacks only a kouloura. It is a paved Court, in front of an elegant West facade of the building, which has the typical recess to indicate the window of a larger room over the storerooms which are immediately behind the West wall (Plate 41). The stronger walls between storerooms 3 and 4, 5 and 6, and 7 and 8 show where the rooms would have been divided on the floor above. Below on the ground, notice the three rock terraces rising in the West wing of the palace from West to East and 7 to the South which has been divided in two by a mud brick wall. In the South-West corner of the palace is a bathroom.

From the Town Court there are steps on the North and North-West into the palace, and by them a very large flat stone with holes. It is a curious object which was perhaps always in this spot, ever since the Minoans settled at Gournia. It could have been used for ritual, and next to it is a small stone with hollows – a rough version of a kernos such as the one at Mallia – which could have had a similar purpose. Inside in the centre is a room which was either a hall or a court, as Evans's assistant Mackenzie pointed out. With its regularly set column bases I think it must have been a court, a small peristyle around an open space. Additional evidence that it is a court is the drain off it to the South, and though there were traces of roof timbers fallen in, they would have had to be 2 m. longer than those at Knossos if the area was a hall. As the excavator remarked, it is far from certain that it was a hall.

The Shrine is a little to the North of the palace, at the end of a lane leading off to the East, the right, from the Main West Road of the town. It measures only 3 × 4 m., and the principal finds were clay tubular stands for bowls or baskets with offerings, and figures of goddesses with raised arms.

Palaikastro

In neither Palaikastro nor Khania has a palace been found, though it is quite possible that at both places they are waiting to be uncovered. They are included with Gournia as they are both Minoan towns of distinctive architecture, whose finds show a standard of living at least as developed as that of the country houses which are described in the next chapter. Palaikastro is remarkable for its elegant main street flanked by several prosperous town houses. At Khania only a little has been excavated, but it is enough to show that it was probably the most important Minoan settlement in West Crete.

On the road from Sitia to Zakro, when you come down to the sea again on the East coast of Crete after leaving Sitia, you will notice a prominent flat topped hill dominating a coastal plain covered with olive trees. The hill is called Kastri and on the plain below is the site of the prosperous Minoan town of Palaikastro. The area was inhabited through almost all of the two millennia of Minoan history, the hill of Kastri being occupied at the beginning and at the end of the era. At both these times its obvious advantages for defence made it worth the effort to settle up there: its defects are that it is very windy and has little water. From Kastri on a clear day you can see the islands of Kasos and Karpathos.

Much of the Minoan town in the plain was excavated, but only a small area has been left uncovered. It is enough however to give an idea of what a rich Minoan town, or at least what its rich quarter was like. The wide streets with their drains, the long and elegant ashlar facades of the houses and the cross roads belong to a more prosperous settlement than Gournia. The wealth of Palaikastro must have come mainly from the excellent agriculture around.

The houses are quite large and airy, and have some similarities with the country houses we shall be looking at later. House B, at the North-East end, has a portico supported by one column opening on to the street. Inside is a peristyle court supported by four columns, like that in the palace at Gournia. On the East side of the house is a larger courtyard, with pillars and column bases to mark a verandah opening on to it. This courtyard may have been a walled garden. The house opposite, House Γ, has another peristyle court, and also has a bath. Along the street to the West is a house with a facade 40 m. long, and at the end is the most recently excavated house in Block N. Here a vestibule leads into an inner hall with a double doorway between. At the back is the largest room, 4.50 m × 5 m., which may have been a dining room, to judge from the evidence of the small pantry off it to the South-East which was packed with four hundred pots. There was an upper floor, as objects had fallen down at an angle. They included two double axes stands and a miniature horns of consecration, which suggests that the house had a shrine on the upper floor.

Khania

On the Kastelli hill on the East side of the town's small harbour recent excavations have begun to reveal the long Minoan history from Khania, from Early Minoan II to Late Minoan IIIB. A few remains of an important building have been left open to view, particularly a fine crazy paving, its stones still polished as they were in Minoan times. It dates from Late Minoan IIIA2 (1375–1300), that is from after the destruction of Knossos when it may be that Khania became the political centre of the island. At this time Khania developed a lively school of pottery whose products you can see in the Khania Museum. Earlier it must have also been important, as a large archive of Linear A tablets and documents has been found.

Khania is blessed with a good harbour, small but sufficient for ancient needs, and some of the most fertile country in Crete in the hinterland. The quality of the finds makes it almost certain that there was a Minoan palace here, or rather several Minoan palaces, of which the latest is probably later than the palace of Knossos. During the thirteenth century (Late Minoan IIIB) it suffered a catastrophic destruction by fire.

Mokhlos and Pseira

Mokhlos and Pseira are two off-shore towns in the Bay of Mirabello. Mokhlos is a small island about 100 m. out to sea from the fishing village of the same name: in Minoan times it may well have been part of Crete, a peninsular. The principal remains at Mokhlos are house-like Early Minoan tombs built against the cliff, which have produced attractive gold jewellery and also the first faience in Crete. In Late Minoan I times there was a quite prosperous settlement, of which you will see some houses by the water's edge where the fishing boat (if you have arranged for one to bring you across from the modern village) will probably land you. Human bones were found in the houses in the debris of the 1450 destruction.

Pseira is another old Minoan settlement. It must always have been an island. You can reach it most easily by tourist boats from Ayios Nikolaos, which may also offer a cruise past (but not stopping off at) Mokhlos. Almost all that you see at Pseira belongs to the Late Minoan I town: houses and the central feature, an impressive long staircase or stepped street, ascending from the inlet where the boats must have come in, to the saddle of the island. A pleasant excursion with good bathing; but remember how bright the sun can be at sea.

11 The Country Houses

The New Palace period country houses are not palaces: they are not so large and they do not have central courts. But the quality of architecture and of the contents of most of them is palatial, and they are equipped with storerooms for farm produce, as are the palaces. They are sited near water supplies and usually have a view over naturally defined areas of countryside which would have been their domains: the houses could see their land and be seen. They seem to have had a similar place in Minoan society to that held by country houses in, say, non-industrial England; but they may also have acted as the local taxation offices – several of them have produced Linear A tablets and sealings made from the same seals as sealings found in the palaces – for the palaces. The palaces would have supplied the houses with luxuries, and the houses would have collected the taxes for the palaces. Some of these houses are set in open countryside and others are in villages which had often existed long before these grand houses were built in them.

The houses all belong to the New Palace period and were mostly built at the end of Middle Minoan III and beginning of Late Minoan I. Many of them were repaired or partly rebuilt during their lifetime, which ended with the fires and destructions of 1450. The principal houses are described below.

Amnisos

The best bathing beach close to Heraklion is about 1 km. to the East of the airport, a long sandy strip with a lush flat valley behind. At the East end of it the old coast road climbs *en corniche* over Kakon Oros ('Bad Mountain') from whose bleak cliffs orange and purple veined breccia was taken by the Minoans for making stone vases. Just before the road starts to climb, it passes a prominent isolated rock by the sea, around which was the Minoan site of Amnisos. One free-standing house has been exposed.

Amnisos was probably one of the harbours of Knossos, another being closer to Heraklion at modern Poros where the Kairatos stream that flows below the palace comes out at the sea. Amnisos occurs as a name in the Linear B tablets and was known in post-Bronze Age times, as early as the *Odyssey*. Also mentioned in the *Odyssey* is the cave of Eileithyia, goddess of childbearing, which has been identified with a sacred cave some 500 m. up the hill to the South behind Amnisos. This cave was used from Late Neolithic till Roman times, and has interesting rock formations and the remains of a terrace where a congregation could have stood to share in the rites. It is worth a visit. Take the side road going inland from opposite the rock of Amnisos and under the new National Road. About 1 km. along the road (which curves), where the ground drops away to

Fig. 13.   Plan of the Palace of Zakro.

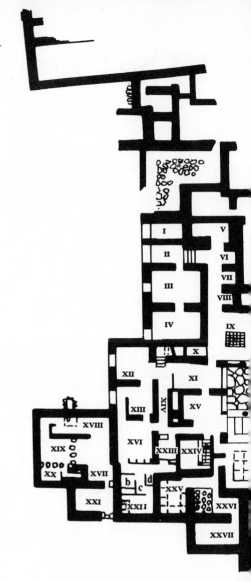

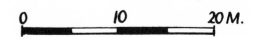

0   10   20 M.

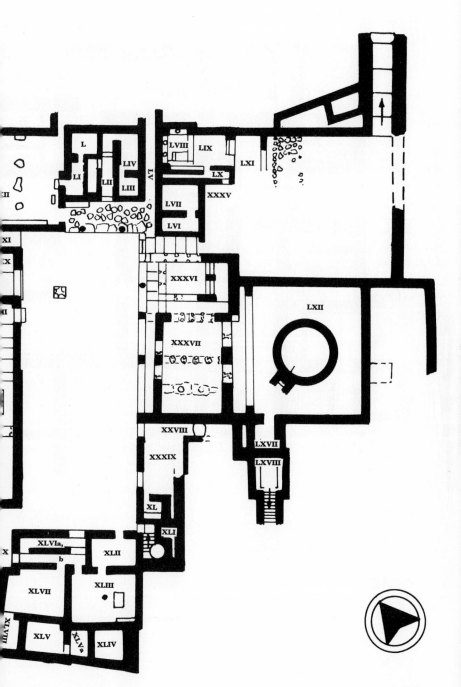

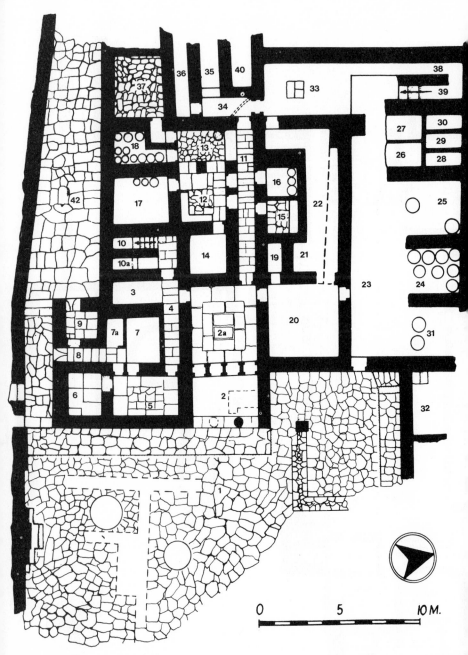

Fig. 14. Plan of the Country House at Nirou Khani.

2a Hall
12 Room of the Benches

the left, is a sign (perhaps faded). Walk down a few metres and a large fig tree marks the entrance of the cave.

Down by the sea the house is on the East side of the rock. It has been called the House of the Lilies from the fresco of lilies, irises and other flowers which was found in the large room on the West side with two column bases. The West wall of the House of the Lilies is made of enormous ashlar blocks on which are mason's marks. The size of the blocks is surprising – the largest is 2.20 m. long – but more surprising is that they have been tipped out of true, sure evidence of a powerful earthquake. If there was one in 1450, it could have caused this; but equally it could be a much later earthquake that moved the stones. There were also many traces of fire, and stones had been thrown down from the upper floor outside the West wall. On the North side is a large room with multiple doors, which opens onto a small schist-paved courtyard. As in the modern *kafenion* below, it would have been pleasant to sit here and enjoy the view out to sea. Equally, when the North wind blows, the double doors of the room would have been essential. The wind can be very strong, and the sea rough.

Scarcely any finds have come from the House of the Lilies, apart from the frescoes. It was probably looted at the time of the disaster, unlike the palace of Zakro whose treasures (or many of them) lay untouched.

Nirou Khani

After leaving Amnisos, the old road to the East climbs over the mountain of Kakon Oros. At the far side it comes down to a mudflat, beyond which the ground rises again to the site of Nirou Khani. Doubtless it was a welcome sight to travellers who had crossed Kakon Oros, as Amnisos would have been to those going the other way.

The house at Nirou Khani (Fig. 14) is one of the finest in Crete. It has splendid views of the sea, and elegant architecture which copies many ideas in the architecture of the palaces. Like Tylissos House A, it is divided into three blocks or wings with an imposing central entrance opening to the East; but it is more compact than Tylissos House A, being placed either side of a central axis, passage 11. There is no obvious bathroom; but perhaps the sea sufficed.

Outside the main entrance is a large paved courtyard 1, part of which is a sidewalk running along the facade of the house. At the South edge of the Court is a small stepped platform on which half of a horns of consecration was found. To the North the smaller court 1a is separated by walls, and this could have been an enclosure for spectators as the platform may have been. Another sidewalk runs along the facade of room 32, and on the South steps take you up to the South Court of the house.

Go through the columns into the vestibule 2 which has a gypsum dado, and on through double doors into the Hall 2a – a typical Minoan contrast between the two columns and three piers (Plate 42). The Hall has three exits, one to each of the three parts of the house. To the South is a passage 4 and off it a dark cubby hole 3 in which a lamp was found. West of 3 the passage leads to the stairs and their return 10 and 10a. You will notice in the passage some particularly clear traces of construction in timber-and-rubble (Plate 43). At the East end of the

42 The entrance to the country house of Nirou Khani may remind you of the grand
West entrance to the palace of Phaistos (Plate 24). The picture is taken from the
courtyard in the foreground; beyond are a Vestibule **2** and the Hall **2a**, faced with
gypsum. Narrow doors lead off from this grand room to the South (the left) and to
the West (straight ahead).

passage is a room **5** with a grey limestone floor bordered by gypsum flagstones,
and off it is **6**, a small room with a divan seat in the corner. Off **5** to the West is a
room divided by a mud brick wall, **7** and **7a**, which is separated from the
passage by another mudbrick wall. In this room four large ceremonial double
axes were found (they are too thin to have been used, and the largest is 1.175 m.
across) and in **7a** a heap of ashes, which led the excavator to think there was a
shrine here, with a fire for cooking sacrificed animals. The short corridor off to
the South is lit by a window opening into the South Court. It takes you into a
small room **9** which also has a window to the outside.

This wing of the house is intricate and private, but we do not know exactly
what it was used for. Perhaps it was the private quarters of the lord of Nirou
Khani and his family.

The central block of the house is more imposing, and its rooms seem to be
intended more for public use. You enter by passage **11** off the North-West
corner of the Hall. Frescoes found in the passage may show part of a goat: the
excavator noted how the frescoes were made. A layer of clay 1 cm. thick was
applied to the stones, on top of which came 2 cm. of clay mixed with straw and
finally the lime plaster (two layers of it here in the passage) which was painted
while still wet – the true fresco technique.

The passage is interrupted by a dividing wall half way along it, which seems
to have been added after the original construction of the house. As it appears
now, you must turn left into the Room of the Benches **12**, the main room in the

43　The evidence of timber-and-rubble construction, the gap where a beam stood, in passage **4** at Nirou Khani. Timber-and-rubble was much used by the Minoans to give buildings a strong but elastic framework to withstand earthquakes. Similar construction can be seen in buildings of the Turkish period in Crete, and the concept is the same as that of the modern use of ferroconcrete.

house. Sit for a while on a bench and notice the contrast between the grey limestone floor and the gypsum flagged passage which separates 12 from the light well at its West end 13. Parts of other benches had fallen in, which must mean that there was another room with benches immediately above, which would have been similarly lit from the light well. Off 12 is an enclosed room where four lamps were found, and to the South you come into 17 and 18 which produced forty to fifty clay three-legged tables of offering, all stacked in piles. There is a third room on the South side 37, which has a crazy paving floor, and a passage back from it behind the light well. On the North side of the Room of the Benches and the light well are two small rooms, 15 and 16: 15 has a built seat, while in 16 three more tables of offering were found like those in the rooms to the South. There are then five excellent rooms grouped around the Room of the Benches, three of which have ritual objects. This led the excavator to call the house at Nirou Khani the 'House of the High Priest', but it is difficult to prove that religious activity here was more than usual for the Minoans.

The two small rooms 15 and 16 are in fact built into the third wing of the house on the North side which you must again reach from the Hall. You pass through room 20 to several storerooms with pithoi on the North edge of the building. At the West end of this wing you will see five mud brick bins inserted into a storeroom, with steps to make it easier to fill them.

Manares

The Minoan country house at Manares is cut through by the modern road from Sitia to Piskokefalo. It is about 2 km. from Sitia, and about 100 m. beyond a very small church-shaped shrine on the side of the road and just before the Klemataria *kafenion*. The house has been terraced into the West side of a rich valley and looks out across it. There is little preserved, and that is obscured by plants. The most distinctive feature is a fine staircase at the North end of the buildings, with an entrance to an upper level, which may have been the main floor of the house. At the bottom of the stairs a thick wall goes East to a projection, or bastion, above the river, and there are remains of what were probably storerooms. It is possible that boats were able to come right up to the house in Minoan times, if it is since then that the present river plain has silted up.

Zou

The house at Zou is in a splendid condition, built (like Manares) into the West slope of the hills overlooking a beautiful and fertile valley which runs off the Piskokefalo valley to the East. It is beside the modern road and is marked by a sign, about 300 m. North of the village of Zou and 0.5 km. up the road from where it leaves the Piskokefalo valley.

The house is simpler than Manares, and may have been nothing more than an isolated farmhouse. It is built mainly of large blocks, with packing stones worked between them. At the South end by the entrance is a small room with a stone bench. Beyond are two deep pits which may have been used for storing corn – they are like the cavities between the walls of the Keep at Knossos – and immediately to the North is a large basement, with two spaces for windows in the North wall. The natural rock slopes down into the basement. The main room of the house would probably have been above.

Ano Zakro

About 1 km. to the South-East of the village of Ano Zakro at a place called Koukou Kefali (Cuckoo's Head) an imposing country house was found recently either side of the road down to Kato Zakro and the palace. It was excavated as part of the programme of work at the palace; some of it cannot be seen, being under the road. The house overlooks, and must have controlled, the fertile and well watered valley below the modern village. It was surely a dependency of the palace, and is built in a similar style, although using more massive blocks. Many fresco fragments were found fallen into the basements which are the only extant remains. They show that it must have been an attractive house, and it was well situated.

Like Zou and Manares, it was built in terraces against the West (more correctly, North-West) slope of the hill, but it was probably a grander house than they were since it was decorated with the frescoes. The basements where the frescoes were found are built of large blocks of grey limestone set against the rocks, though there is also some ashlar masonry. Some of these ashlar blocks are plastered on the outside with white lime plaster and between the joints, a stucco technique which has not been found in the palace at Kato Zakro.

The basement to the East has a central pillar. Some plaster was still in position on the walls, and more had fallen from the room above. The basement contained eight pithoi, one of which had a Linear A inscription on the shoulder. The room next to it, where stones and plaster had fallen from an upper floor, is on the same level as the large room to the South in which a double wine press was found, the best from Minoan Crete except perhaps for that at Vathypetro. In two other small rooms is a stone conduit which brought water from a nearby spring.

The wine press is some evidence of the agricultural resources of Ano Zakro, but olives may have been even more important, to judge by the number of trees you see in the area today. There is no archaeological evidence of large-scale olive production at either Ano Zakro or down at the palace, but it is quite possible then that oil contributed as much to the importance of the Zakro area as the goods from abroad which I have suggested were received at the palace harbour. These goods would have passed the house at Ano Zakro on their way to the centre of the island.

Vathypetro

Vathypetro is a large country house built on a promontory overlooking a long and deep East-West valley typical of the landscape of inland Central Crete. It is set in a superb situation with stupendous views across to Psiloriti to the West and the great double rock of Kanli Kastelli in the middle distance and on the South to the passes that lead to the Mesara plain and Phaistos. The country around is well watered and fertile, and the house is conveniently close to Arkhanes and Knossos.

Take the road going South out of the village of Arkhanes and continue along it at the foot of Mount Iouktas (a road turns off to the right to take you up the mountain for the view and to visit the Minoan peak sanctuary) to a low pass or saddle. There follow the road around to the East (to the left) and in a few hundred metres you will see the restored buildings of Vathypetro about 200 m. off the road to the South, your right. There is a water tap at the spot where you leave the road to walk to the house through vineyards.

The house has been published only in preliminary reports, and there is no comprehensive plan available. The building is aligned North-South; and the main entrance, like that of Nirou Khani, is from a courtyard on the East through three columns. The bases of these columns, you will notice, are of different stones: conglomerate, breccia and veined limestone. Opposite the entrance across the small courtyard is a ruined building, which has a central recess flanked by two built squares with hollow centres. It is almost certainly a three-part shrine, like that in the miniature frescoes of Knossos. The central recess reminds you of the sacred seats or offering tables in recesses in the House of the Chancel Screen and in the Royal Villa at Knossos. The recess here at Vathypetro could have held either a seat, or a statue which may have been of wood and looked like the half-lifesize clay statues of Minoan goddesses from Ayia Irini on Kea. The hollows that flank the recess might have contained double axe stands, like those at Knossos, or – more likely – flagstaffs, which you can see flanking a shrine on the Mountain Shrine Rhyton from Zakro.

The rest of the East facade is elegantly built in ashlar with recesses for windows. At the South-East corner is another entrance leading into an open air corridor beside the storerooms which have been roofed over. The main surviving room here, like the large storerooms against the West side, is a basement pillar room, built in the same way as the pillar basements in the West side of the palace and in the South House at Knossos. Wine presses were found in this room; and beyond the two small adjoining storerooms to the West were the stairs to the floor which this pillar basement indicates was certainly above. The passage from the South-East corner entrance leads into a room, which may have been a light area, North of these stairs; and from here you enter a large room with a schist crazy paving floor, and with four pillars.

The large storeroom on the West is also roofed over. It was reached from the main entrance. On the way one passed a small built receptacle, perhaps intended for treasures. At the back of it is a recess in the West facade of the house where there may have been another shrine approached from the West Court, which might be compared with that on the West Court at Mallia.

The West Court of Vathypetro is paved. Notice the large oil press, the drains coming out of the wall and the remains of outbuildings or sheds built against the house.

The North part of the house may have had the living and reception rooms. They are not easy to make out, as there are two periods of building and the earlier walls are exposed as well as the later ones, even in the main hall of the house. From the South-West corner of the main hall you can enter a passage and go North by a dogleg passage to a rectangular room at the North-West which may have been a bathroom. This passage also takes you South into a fine pillared storeroom. The West wall of this room is a retaining wall and maybe built recently but, if so, it is in the position of the ancient wall. At the bottom of this wall a drain comes out of the storerooms, perhaps for taking away waste water after they had been swabbed down. Notice that the storerooms are on a level 1.5 m. lower, built where the ground already begins to drop away.

Vathypetro is important for its details, and for the fact that so much evidence of ancient agriculture has been preserved. It is a pity that it has never been properly published and that the rooms which have been roofed are locked up. If this were not so, it would be given more attention by archaeologists and by the public, as it deserves.

Mitropolis

The house at Mitropolis is in the Mesara plain. To reach it, at a locality called Kannia, take the side road to the East (left) off the main road from Heraklion to Phaistos, after leaving the village of Ayii Dheka and before reaching the Gortyn basilica.

The house was built basically as one block, with a large number of store-rooms containing pithoi. It was destroyed with almost every other centre in Crete around 1450 in Late Minoan IB but was later inhabited again. The most interesting finds from it probably belong to this late period of use: clay goddesses with raised arms (known in Late Minoan IIIB and IIIC, the thirteenth and twelfth centuries, from other sites in Crete) and clay tubular stands for supporting baskets or bowls with offerings to be set before the goddesses.

Tylissos

To the South-West of Heraklion is the fertile area of Malevisi, which has been known for centuries for its wine. In the Middle Ages it was shipped from Heraklion (Candia) to Monemvasia in the Peloponnese and thence to Western Europe. The wine was sold as Malmsey, and a Duke of Clarence was drowned in it.

In the West half of Malevisi is a Minoan settlement by the modern village of Tylissos. Tylissos is on the West side of a shallow valley and on the route to Psiloriti (or Mount Ida) from Knossos and Heraklion. Three houses have been excavated, one of which (B) is rather simple: the other two (A, C) are as grand as the houses at Nirou Khani and Vathypetro, although, being side by side, it is possible they formed part of a prosperous town such as Palaikastro and should not really be classed with Nirou Khani and Vathypetro as country houses.

House A

House A (Fig. 15) is that at the South-East of the excavation area of Tylissos. It is entered from the South-East through a typical dogleg passage which leads into a

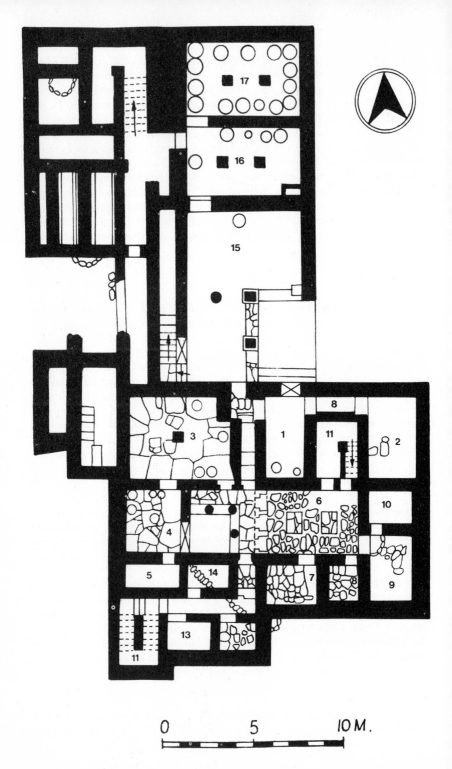

Fig. 15. Plan of Tylissos House A

44   Room **6** (in the foreground) of Tylissos House A was lit by a light well, as was room **4** behind through the window. The ashlar is of fine quality at Tylissos: notice that the line of the North edge of the light well (to the left of the two column bases) is continued up the West wall.

court around which the house is built, almost in the Elizabethan fashion of an E with its middle cut out. On the West and North of the court is a peristyle, with stairs rising on the West and a window lighting the staircase; another window lights a room on the South of the court.

A passage leads North from the peristyle to two large storerooms. You will notice in the further storeroom that the pithoi on the North side rest on stone slabs while those on the South are set in the ground. Those on the North also have bung holes near their bases and must have held oil, while the others would have been for corn.

The South wing of House A is the more interesting half of the building. A passage takes you to room **6** which faces onto a light well with a window opening on to it from the West (Plate 44). At its South-West corner notice the drain. Room **3** to the North is a pillar crypt or basement: a pyramidal stand for a double axe was found in it (similar to those by the Storerooms at Knossos: Plate 15), while off it are two rooms **4** and **5** which may have been treasuries. From **4** or near to it came three enormous bronze cauldrons, a chance find which were the clue to the Minoan settlement. In **4** the usual vertical and horizontal holes in the walls for wooden beams show up particularly well.

South of the light well a passage leads to a staircase and its return. To the East grouped around **6** are several rooms, including a bath **11**.

Tylissos House A is remarkable for the quality of its building, the excellence of its ashlar work, and for the fact that so many windows have been preserved.

45　The Late Minoan III house over House C at Tylissos included a cistern with drains leading into it. Only a few cisterns have been found from Minoan Crete; you can see others at Zakro and Pyrgos.

House C

House C to the North of House A has the remains of a Late Minoan III house built over it about 1 m. higher. These remains include a column base (though two other column bases are, I think, Classical, to judge from the way their surfaces have been dressed) and a large cistern with the drains to fill it (Plate 45). You will see that the level of the top of the cistern clearly belongs with the level of the Late Minoan III house, and hence that the cistern cannot possibly be part of the New Palace period House C. This later house was probably built around a large hall (or *megaron*) with vestibule and porch and ancillary rooms. This design of building was more common in mainland Greece and could have been introduced to Crete during or after the period of Mycenaean rule at Knossos (1450–1375).

The earlier House C is well preserved, though it is not as interesting a design as House A. It is basically square and was entered from the East where two wings form a court. Its main room is similar to room **6** in House A: a hall opening onto a light well with living rooms around. The storerooms are on the West and to the South is a pillar room with what was probably a treasury beside it.

Sklavokambos

If you continue past Tylissos towards the village of Anoyia (from where you can reach the high plain of Nidha and the Idaean Cave, a Minoan sacred cave on Psiloriti) you climb up through a steep valley into a small open plain, called

Sklavokambos. About halfway along the plain the road passes immediately beside the remains of a Minoan country house on the left. The house is placed just above the plain on the edge of the foothills, and would certainly have been the local ruling house.

Sklavokambos is crudely built, and lacks the niceties of the houses at Tylissos. No trace even of a built floor or pavement was found, which means that they would have been of beaten earth. All the same it is still worth looking at, as another example of the skill of the Minoan planners even in such simple circumstances. It is aligned North-South, with a verandah at the North end offering a view over the plain, an arrangement like that at Amnisos beside the sea. Inside the rooms are well laid out: the private rooms were probably on the North-East, and there are storerooms containing pithoi behind the verandah to the North; while to the South are the more public rooms, which include a peristyle court (a smaller version of that at Phaistos, perhaps), which uses three pillars with the South-West corner of an adjacent room as the fourth to support the roof over the cloister, leaving the centre open to light and air.

The main entrance is from the East, which leads into the private wing, if it is that, on the North side. In the entrance passage several clay sealings were found, with impressions made from gold signet rings engraved mostly with scenes of bull-leaping. Impressions from the same seals have been identified at Zakro, Gournia and Ayia Triadha, which is probably an indication of how the Minoans' administration worked. A man must have travelled around to the local centres carrying the ring, to seal whatever needed sealing with the mark of a higher authority. The man presumably came from Knossos.

Monastiraki

The Amari valley is a well watered and secret valley to the West of Psiloriti, running in a North-East – South-West direction across the centre of Crete. It is the easiest route between the North coast in the West of the island and Phaistos and the Mesara on the South. Near the village of Monastiraki and just South of an imaginary line between the village and that of Vistayi on the opposite side of the valley and on a saddle immediately to the North-West of the prominent rock of Kharakas are walls, which may be the remains of a Minoan country house. They are made of massive blocks, crudely shaped. The building is in a commanding position above the valley and has a fine view of Psiloriti.

Pyrgos

On the East side of the river Myrtos, opposite the modern village of Myrtos, the hill of Pyrgos is crowned by a country house which has recently been excavated. It is a steep, but short, walk up the hill, and well worthwhile for the splendid views the house commanded and for the excellence of its architecture.

The house faces North and South. To the South it overlooks the Libyan Sea; to the North it has been carefully aligned on the rich valley of the river Myrtos that runs up towards the Lasithi mountains which encircle the horizon. About 1 km. inland you can see an arched Venetian bridge carrying the old road from

46   The courtyard and South front of the country house at Pyrgos. Much of the
building has been destroyed, but the contrasts of the courtyard are preserved: crazy
paving, a raised walk of flagstones and borders of purple limestones to the walk and a
verandah behind it and to a pavilion or shrine in the left foreground. On the far edge
of the courtyard is a pool (originally a Middle Minoan cistern, which was filled with
pebbles when the courtyard was laid out), which was fed by drains from the house.
Perhaps it was planted with lilies?

Heraklion, Knossos and Central Crete to the East of the island across the river.
This is an ancient route which at this point comes down off the mountains to sea
level; doubtless a consideration when the Minoan country house was built.

On the top of the hill you come to the courtyard and South front of the house
(Plate 46). A circular pool at the South-West corner of the courtyard was a
soakaway for stormwater from the house (drains were found leading to it
outside the West wall of the house), and it may have been planted with flowers.
It was originally a Middle Minoan cistern, over 2 m. deep and holding some 23
tonnes of water, which was filled with river pebbles when the court was laid
out. There is another, and much larger, Middle Minoan cistern of about 70
tonnes' capacity on the North slope of Pyrgos.

Facing onto the courtyard are the country house and, to the East, a small
pavilion or shrine. This building is mostly destroyed; but you can still see where
the back and side walls were, and there is a column base in front with an edging
of purple limestones onto the courtyard. These stones come from the mountains nearby. They are also used between the raised walk that crosses the
courtyard and the country house's verandah behind. The verandah has a central
pillar, two purple column bases and a floor of gypsum, now cut by pits made in
the last century to quarry the ashlar masonry. Above the verandah we can
imagine that there was a balcony for the grand rooms on the first floor.

47 The light well, bench and staircase at Pyrgos. The bench is of gypsum: its triglyph decoration imitates carved wood. The floor below may have been of wood, which has rotted: this would be more in keeping with the elegance of the suite than the rock you see now. The door beside the bench leads into a small pantry cut out of the rock.

At the South-West corner of the house is the main entrance. A little along the entrance passage a door on the right leads into three basements cut out of the rock, onto which the gypsum slabs of the first floor had fallen. Back in the passage the remains of a household shrine had fallen on these slabs a little beyond the door to the basements. Lying on the gypsum were a Linear A tablet recording ninety units of wine (Plate 9), two clay sealings, a conch shell of pink faience and four clay tubular stands for offerings: a typically Minoan mixture of religion and the economy.

The entrance passage leads to a light well, also with a floor of the purple limestones, here pointed with white plaster. The floor slopes from its corners towards a central basin which collected the rain. It may be, since this light well is unusual in having walls of gypsum rather than ashlar, that the gypsum was protected by overhanging eaves which sent the rain straight into the basin. Facing the light well is an elegant gypsum bench, with triglyph decoration imitating carved wood (Plate 47). By contrast the floor of the passage below the bench is nothing more than the cut rock, but it was probably originally of wood which would match the quality of the rest of the architecture. Beside the bench is a pantry cut out of the rock. It contained a large storage jar and stacks of cups. Its threshold of gypsum is built with a keystone to hold the sides in position.

A gypsum staircase beside the light well goes up to the first floor rooms. The whole of this part of the house is cut out of the rock, so that the first floor would have been about on the level of the rock at the top of the hill: this would have made it easy to support yet another floor above. Such an extra floor would have enjoyed the view up the valley from the North edge of the hill. The staircase is an elegant construction, with a parapet to separate it from the light well. The parapet is stepped and had a wooden column at the end of each step, to hold either the floor above or the return of the staircase. The top course of each step of the parapet was supported by wooden sleepers, which have now rotted, which explains why each top course has split apart. At the bottom of the stairs is a stone basin, a stoup or a flower pot. Little was found in this area except a dried fig and a fragment of a vase made of obsidian from Yiali in the Dodecanese – nothing more than a fragment but, being only the tenth vase known of this material from the whole Minoan world, an indication of the riches the house once contained. These riches can be observed equally in the architecture of Pyrgos – the tight and clever use of a small space which, with the buildings cut from the rock, the light well, stepped parapet and staircase, is almost a miniature of the Grand Staircase of Knossos.

The East wing of the house has an ashlar facade facing onto a street which runs up the hill from the houses of the Late Minoan I village on the East slope, and joins the raised walk of the courtyard. Vases had fallen onto the street from an upper room: two Cycladic jugs, a stirrup jar (for oil?) and two curious rhyta with elaborate handles and painted decoration to imitate similar vases of marble. The upper room(s) would have been over two storerooms behind the ashlar facade: their walls are finished with mud plaster – a contrast to the outside. In the storerooms were pithoi containing carbonised barley and bitter vetch, and greasy earth which should indicate oil: combustible produce, which explains why the rooms and the pithoi were badly burnt. The storerooms are reached from a passage from the street, the second entrance to the house, which continues to other rooms to the North. The passage may have originally been open, as it is paved in the same way as the street outside and it has a runnel for water on its East side. The stone construction at the North end of the larger storeroom may have been a loading platform, or a staircase to the upper floor.

The house at Pyrgos is notable for its setting and its architecture, its tight plan which makes best use of the natural rock, its gypsum and ashlar masonry, and its use of colour and contrast in the floors and courtyard. Here we shall end our tour of the Minoan palaces, towns and country houses.

12 After the Palaces

Around the middle of the fifteenth century a more serious disaster than any observed hitherto afflicted Minoan Crete. All the palaces (except Knossos) and the towns, including parts of Knossos, and the country houses were destroyed. By contrast with previous disasters, this time the Minoans did not stay on to start building again. Either they fled into the mountains or they perished in the troubles. To judge from the archaeological record, the social order in the provinces for a time was smashed. The palaces and houses had been burnt and looted, and people in their fright had left the tools of their trade uncollected from where they had hidden them. In the town on the island of Mokhlos human bones were noticed in the debris.

I have suggested that invading Mycenaeans brought this havoc, sparing the palace of Knossos which eventually was itself destroyed about 1375 (p. 48). Gradually, settled life returned to Crete in the period between the disasters, and the quality of the material objects – the pottery or the bronze vases for instance – changed little, as they were presumably still being made by the same families or groups of Minoan craftsmen as before. But, as you can see in the now explored 'Unexplored Mansion' at Knossos, the people, presumably Mycenaean nobles, for whom the objects were being made had less concern than their Minoan predecessors for the quality of life. In the elegant main room of that grand house, small stone partitions were built and fires lit against them – camping or, in Evans's term, squatting.

Why Knossos was destroyed about 1375 is even more difficult to explain than why the other palaces and country houses had been destroyed about three quarters of a century earlier. The Thera volcano had erupted long before; an earthquake is always possible: but I think it more likely that it was again humans who created the disaster. The islanders could have revolted, particularly if authority in Crete was now no longer dispersed but was so centralised in Knossos that the Mycenaeans had in effect become absentee landlords for the provinces, with all that that entails. Or pirates could have raided Knossos. Or, as in later times Venice had trouble with the independently minded Venetian nobles of Crete, so perhaps Mycenaeans from the mainland came to destroy the palace, resenting its still strong power: Knossos, I think, controlled the Aegean's connections with the East Mediterranean until its destruction. This theory of an attack from the mainland is the more attractive as it is the one that can be best linked to what happened immediately after Knossos was destroyed, when Mycenaean (mainland) trade with the East Mediterranean suddenly flowered. It can also explain the growth of Mycenaean control of the islands of the South Aegean, which are on the direct route from the Argolid and Attica to the East. Knossos had to be destroyed.

The collapse of the Minoan palaces in the period 1450–1375 was not the end of the Minoan culture, which continued for another four hundred years until about 970 when the Early Iron Age can be said to have begun in Crete. Our knowledge of this period after the palaces is not as great as that of the New Palace period but it is growing, as new excavations produce more evidence.

Though the palace of Knossos was in ruins, the palatial system may not have broken down completely if a palace was still flourishing, or if a new palace was built, at Khania. The evidence is sketchy but the quality of the finds there and the quality of the extant architecture suggest that the centre of Cretan power may have been moved from Knossos to Khania, and that there may have been a palace there after 1375. Elsewhere life carried on much as it had done before. People were still living on flat, low-lying places, and nothing suggests that there was any threat of attack. Crete may have been under a loose Mycenaean control from the mainland, but this is far from certain: the culture is still peculiarly Cretan. If Crete did seem dangerous to the Mycenaeans, it would have been less so than before as there were fewer settlements, as far as we know, and the population had probably fallen. Only at Khania were there fairly close links with mainland Greece.

This state of affairs lasted through Late Minoan IIIA2 (1375–1300) into Late Minoan IIIB (1300–1200) until, at the end of the thirteenth century, even Crete became involved in the turmoils which broke out throughout the East Mediterranean. During the thirteenth century parts of the ruined palaces of Knossos and Phaistos had been cleared out and reinhabited, and the Shrine of the Double Axes at Knossos was inaugurated. It is odd that in this period we know more of the religious practices and habits of burial than we do of life in the settlements: for the Late Minoan I heyday of the New Palaces, the reverse is true. A favourite method of burial in Late Minoan III was in clay coffins, either box-like with a pointed roof or lid, or bath-shaped. Both types are painted with octopuses, fishes, birds and flowers, and some have hunting scenes. The finest *larnax*, a Greek word meaning chest or coffer, can be seen in the Ierapetra Museum. (Found before the war, it has not yet been published.)

As for Late Minoan III religion, we know of shrines with benches such as the Shrine of the Double Axes at Knossos or the Shrine at Gournia, and of clay statues of goddesses with raised arms to whom the offerings were made. The idea of a shrine with a bench at the back wall already existed in the time of the New Palaces: that at Ayia Triadha is an example, which was re-used in Late Minoan IIIB. Some of the offerings in them were probably placed in bowls or baskets which were set on clay tubular stands and stood before the bench. Such shrines with clay goddesses and stands were still venerated in the last period of Minoan civilisation, Late Minoan IIIC (1200–970). In one shrine of that period the crown of the goddess was decorated with modelled heads of the opium poppy.

Our knowledge of what happened in Crete at the end of the thirteenth century is fragmentary. It was clearly a time of movement, discord and danger: twice, groups of people seem to have come to invade, or to settle, from mainland Greece. They may have been refugees from the contemporary disasters there. The first arrivals have been detected from the appearance of new ideas in pottery, such as a deep and rather globular bowl (the 'deep bowl') which had been current on the mainland for a century. The second arrivals are shown by other changes: cremating the dead, a greater though still rare use of iron, and the use of fibulae or safety pins and of long pins to hold women's dresses, which indicate a change of fashion and probably a change of the people who wore them. At the same time as these people could have been coming from the mainland, new settlements were founded on remote peaks, at any rate in the East of the island, which suggests that the newcomers drove out the native Minoans or that the Minoans often fled in their path. At Palaikastro, for example, the bleak hill of Kastri was inhabited again for the first time since the third millennium. In the centre of Crete however there was apparently less disturbance at places such as Phaistos and Knossos. Knives and weapons of Italian type are other evidence of change (were they brought in trade? or in war? by mercenaries?), and a new school developed of painting octopuses on stirrup jars which flourished in Crete, on the East coast of Attica and in the islands of the Cyclades and the Dodecanese. This grouping of cultural influences across the southern Aegean at the end of the Bronze Age corresponds surprisingly closely to that of the Minoan influence or control of Late Minoan I. Outside the Aegean, some Minoan traits appeared in the eleventh-century pottery of Cyprus along with many more Mycenaean traits. Mycenaeans had certainly settled in Cyprus from the twelfth century; in the eleventh Minoans may have joined them.

In the succeeding centuries of transition from Bronze Age to Archaic and Classical Greece the Minoan tradition did not completely disappear. When you look at Cretan Protogeometric (970–820) and Geometric (820–700) vases, you can still see motifs of Minoan ancestry; clay figurines of bulls, goddesses and houses or shrines were still made as they had been in Late Minoan IIIB or IIIC: and, as further evidence of the strength of the Minoan religious tradition, the sacred cave of Psykhro in the Lasithi mountains was venerated for about a thousand years, from the beginning of the New Palace period in Middle Minoan III until the seventh century. In the eight and seventh centuries when seals began to be used again, Minoan gems were picked up in the fields – as they still are today – and were used or sometimes copied. At this time came the first surviving references to a heroic Cretan past in the *Iliad* and the *Odyssey*, memories perhaps of Bronze Age Crete.

Later, in the fifth century, Thucydides described Minos at the beginning of his history as the man who ruled the sea and cleared it of pirates, a forerunner of Pericles and Periclean Athens who ruled the same sea. His Minos was that of Homer and tradition, a man like King Arthur in Britain; but, as we have seen, there is some archaeological, that is non-literary, basis in Late Minoan I for the exploits, if not for the man. Late Minoan I, before the mid-fifteenth century destructions, was the time of widest influence of the most individual culture in the long history of the great island of Crete.

The acme of this culture came with the Old and the New Palaces. The palaces and the life that was lived in and around them are the essence of Minoan civilisation, as I hope I have explained. To separate one period from the other, to claim that the culture of Minoan Crete reached higher levels in one or the other, is invidious or irrelevant. I prefer the art of the Old Palaces, which consists principally of its Kamares ware vases, but this is of course a personal judgement; others prefer the art of the New Palaces: some even believe that Cretan culture was at its peak when the disasters came in 1450, a view that cannot be proved since we cannot tell how things would have developed if there had been no disasters. Most remarks about the Minoans will be found to say more of the people who make them than of the Minoans.

These difficulties have not deterred many from trying to rationalise Minoan civilisation. Cretan influence in the Aegean has been stressed by those interested in ideas of empire and navy, as some scholars in modern Britain, or Thucydides in fifth-century Athens. Others emphasise the importance of women, whether goddesses or priestesses, and certainly the apparent lack of a male deity is surprising when we think of the later pre-eminence of Zeus. What I notice most about the Minoans are: their appreciation of nature in the placing of their buildings and in the representation of nature in their frescoes; a quiet humour, as in the crowd scenes in the miniature frescoes or in the depiction of animals and fish; a love of form and complexity, and an understanding of what refreshment these can bring (by contrast with nature); and their enjoyment of the oblique and unobvious – the dogleg approach, the grand entrance dissolving into the small exit. There is not much more I can say. The Minoans seem to have had such a strong culture that we are impressed and intrigued, and we long to know what is behind it and what their thoughts were. These are things we can never know. There is no Minoan literature preserved, and all the excavations of Crete remedy only a little of that lack. We can only use our imaginations to recreate the Minoans' sensibilities.

Glossary

Ashlar	Squared hewn stone, usually in regular courses (ashlar masonry).
Bath	Interior room, usually sunken, probably used for cleansing (in the Minoan palaces this could have been as much a spiritual as a physical operation). Often known as *lustral basin*.
Carbon-14 dating	Also known as *radiocarbon dating*. A method of dating organic materials by measuring their Carbon-14 content that remains after death: half will have been lost after 5730 years (the *half-life*).
Cist	Stone-lined box, or cavity, set in the floor.
Country house	Substantial house built in the country, the ruling house of a locality. Sometimes known as *villa*.
Dado	Lining of (the lower part of) a wall. In Minoan Crete, usually of *gypsum*.
Gypsum	Hydrous sulphate of calcium, a white to buff limestone that can be easily sawn and polished. Used by the Minoans as marble was later, both for blocks and as a lining, or veneer, for walls of other material (see dado).
Horns of consecration	Stylized bull's horns, found in shrines and shown in frescoes on the eaves of buildings. Preserved examples are usually of plaster or stone.
Keep	Used of the Keeps **13** at Knossos and **V** (*le Donjon*) at Mallia, both of stout construction reminding their excavators of the keeps of mediaeval castles.
Kernos	A Greek word, now used for dishes of stone or clay with small receptacles for offerings.
Kouloura	A Greek word referring to things that are round and hollow: in Minoan Crete, the built pits in the West Courts of Knossos, Phaistos and Mallia which may have been used for storing grain, or possibly for receiving sacred offerings.
Light well	Shaft giving light and ventilation to interior rooms.
Lustral basin	See *bath*.
'Magazine'	An out-of-date term for a storeroom.
Megaron	A Greek word for a hall. Used in Aegean Bronze Age archaeology for a hall, often having a central hearth, with only one entrance through a porch on one side (found in mainland Greece and elsewhere).
Mud brick	Brick of sun-dried earth or clay (sometimes fired accidentally in the destruction of a building).
Orthostat	Block of stone appearing set upright (rather than on its side).
Palace	Administrative, economic, social, religious and cultural centre in Minoan Crete; official residence perhaps of royalty, priest-royalty or priests and/or priestesses.
Peristyle	Colonnade surrounding a central open area; cloister.

Pillar basement, pillar crypt	Underground or ground floor room with pillar(s) to support room(s) above. *Pillar crypt* is used to refer to a room that seems to have had a religious use.
Propylon (propylaeum –a)	In Classical Greece, entrance to a temple or shrine; in Minoan Crete, ceremonial entrance to a palace or country house, porch with one or more columns.
Raised walk	Raised flagstone walk crossing a courtyard. Sometimes known as 'causeway'.
Tree-ring corrections	Also known as *dendrochronological calibration*. A method of adjusting errors in *Carbon-14 dating* by calibrating dates according to correction factors derived from comparing the Carbon-14 dates of the rings of long-lived trees with the calendrical dates obtained by counting the rings.
Triglyph	Block with three vertical grooves (or two whole grooves and a half-groove each side): in Minoan Crete found as part of gypsum benches.
Villa	See *country house*.

Select Bibliography

General

S. Alexiou, *Minoan Civilisation* (Heraklion 1969). A good introduction.
J. W. Graham, *The Palaces of Crete* (Princeton 2nd ed. 1969). A pioneering work in elucidating the principles of reconstructing Minoan buildings.
R. Higgins, *Minoan and Mycenaean Art* (London and New York 1967).
S. Hood, *The Minoans* (London and New York 1971). The best general account, sometimes heretical.
R. W. Hutchinson, *Prehistoric Crete* (Harmondsworth and Baltimore 1962). Stimulating.
S. Marinatos and M. Hirmer, *Crete and Mycenae* (London and New York 1960). Good pictures and interesting text.
J. D. S. Pendlebury, *The Archaeology of Crete* (London 1939; reprinted). Still virtually the only textbook.
J. W. Shaw, *Minoan Architecture: Materials and Techniques (Annuario della Scuola Archeologica di Atene* 49 (1971); Rome 1973). An excellent new account of how Minoan buildings were built.

Guides, etc.

Knossos, Phaistos and Mallia:
S. Alexiou, *A Guide to the Minoan Palaces: Knossos-Phaestos-Mallia* (Heraklion n.d.). Good.

Knossos

A. J. Evans, *The Palace of Minos at Knossos* 1–4 with Index (London 1921–1935; reprinted). Still indispensable. A good read. Baroque style.
J. D. S. Pendlebury, *A Handbook to the Palace of Minos at Knossos* (London paperback ed. 1954). Lively.

Phaistos and Ayia Triadha

L. Pernier and L. Banti, *Guida degli Scavi Italiani in Creta* (Rome 1947). Dated.
D. Levi, *The Recent Excavations at Phaistos* (Lund 1964).

Mallia

C. Tiré and H. van Effenterre, *Guide des Fouilles Françaises en Crète* (Paris 1966). Excellent.

Zakro

N. Platon, *Zakros* (New York and London 1971).

Gournia

J. W. Graham, 'The Cretan Palace: Sixty-Seven Years of Exploration', in *A Land Called Crete* (Smith College, Massachusetts 1968) 17–44.

Index